Core Jail Standards

FOUNDED 1870

American Correctional Association
206 N. Washington St., Suite 200
Alexandria, VA 22314
(800) 222-5646
www.aca.org

Mission of the American Correctional Association

The American Correctional Association provides a professional organization for all individuals and groups, both public and private, that share a common goal of improving the justice system.

Photos on cover: Courtesy of Rod Miller, Mackinac County, Michigan, Sheriff's Office and Jail

American Correctional Association Staff

Harold W. Clarke, President
James A. Gondles, Jr., CAE, Executive Director
Gabriella M. Klatt, Director, Communications and Publications
Alice Heiserman, Manager of Publications and Research
Jeannelle Ferreira, Associate Editor
Leigh Ann Bright, Graphics and Production Associate
Cover by Leigh Ann Bright

Printed in the United States of America by Versa Press, East Peoria, Ill.

ISBN: 978-56991-315-4

For information on publications and videos available from ACA, contact our worldwide web home page at: www.aca.org

This publication may be ordered from:
American Correctional Association
206 N. Washington St., Suite 200
Alexandria, VA 22314
(800) 222-5646 ext. 0129

Library of Congress Cataloging in Publication Data
American Correctional Association.
 Core jail standards / American Correctional Association.
  p. cm.
 ISBN 978-1-56991-315-4
 1. Jails--Standards--United States. 2. Jails--Administration--Standards--United States. I. Title.
 HV8746.U6A46 2010
 365'.9730218--dc22
           2009041380

CONTENTS

Part Three: Order

Part Four: Care

Part Five: Program and Activity

Part Six: Justice

Part Seven: Administration and Management

Foreword

The Core Jail Standards in this manual were developed with all of America's jails, regardless of size, in mind. Having been a sheriff and having managed a jail, I am particularly pleased with this manual's relevance to small- and medium-sized facilities. These standards are the work product of corrections practitioners, particularly those employed in jails. With the support of the American Jail Association, National Sheriffs' Association, National Institute of Corrections (NIC), and the Federal Bureau of Prisons these standards have been evaluated and tested and represent sound jail operational policies.

ACA's standards are guidelines for the improvement of correctional operations and programs. They provide a national framework for presenting the needs and concerns of correctional agencies to correctional administrators, legislators, funding bodies, and the public. They set levels of compliance for correctional facilities seeking to upgrade their services, programs, and operations.

With this manual, the nation gains a comprehensive set of minimum jail standards. The strengths and practicality of the standards presented in this book are a testament to the more than thirty corrections professionals who participated in their development, and to the facilities that rigorously field tested the standards. These standards will enable jails of all sizes to improve operational effectiveness and efficiency and help to make our country's jails more safe for the community, the staff, and the inmates.

For those agencies that would like to receive an independent assessment of compliance with these standards, ACA offers a "certification" process that is similar to its accreditation process. More information about certification is provided at the end of this manual.

There are many resources available to help those who want to implement these standards. NIC can offer guidance and assistance. The *Performance-Based Standards for Adult Local Detention Facilities* published by ACA, from which these core standards were developed, can provide more information about many of the core standards and expected practices.

Jail standards at the state and national level have guided the improvement of jails for more than thirty years. I encourage jails of all sizes to adopt these core standards, subject themselves to independent assessment to ensure compliance, and seek certification.

James A. Gondles, Jr., CAE
Executive Director
American Correctional Association

Participants in the Core Jail Standards Development Process

Jim Barbee, program specialist, National Institute of Corrections

Jeffrey Beard, secretary, Pennsylvania Department of Corrections

Ron Budzinski, FAIA, president, PSA-Dewberry

Nancy Elmer, manager, Regional Clinical Programs, Correctional Medical Services

Mark Flowers, detention director, ICA-Farmville

Stanley Glanz, sheriff, Tulsa County (Okla.) Sheriff's Office

James A. Gondles, Jr., executive director, American Correctional Association

Elizabeth Gondles, Ph.D., president, Institute for Criminal Justice Healthcare

David Haasenritter, assistant deputy, Corrections Oversight, Army Review Board Agency

Jamie Haight, chief, Program Analysis Section, Federal Bureau of Prisons

Robert Hall, captain, Grand Traverse County (Mich.) Sheriff's Office

Sid Hamberlin, captain, Bonneville County (Idaho) Sheriff's Office

Jim Hart, chief of corrections, Hamilton County (Tenn.) Sheriff's Office

Leslee Hunsicker, health care administrator, American Correctional Association

Virginia Hutchinson, chief, Jails Division, National Institute of Corrections

Newton Kendig, M.D., assistant director, Health Services Division, Federal Bureau of Prisons

Harley Lappin, director, Federal Bureau of Prisons

Lannette Linthicum, M.D., director, Health Services Division, Texas Department of Criminal Justice

John May, M.D. chief medical officer, Armor Correctional Health Services

Rod Miller, president, CRS, Inc.

David Parrish, former jail commander, Hillsborough County (Fla.) Sheriff's Office

Gwyn Smith-Ingley, executive director, American Jail Association

Everette VanHoesen, sheriff, Kay County (Okla.) Sheriff's Office

David Ward, captain, Frederick County (Md.) Detention Center

Jeffrey Washington, deputy executive director, American Correctional Association

FOUNDATION/CORE STANDARDS FOR JAILS

Total Number of Standards: 138

Mandatory Standards: 45
Non-Mandatory Standards: 93

Summary of Mandatory Core Standards

1-CORE-1A-01	Sanitation	1-CORE-4D-04	Personnel Qualifications/Credentials
1-CORE-1A-02	Sanitation	1-CORE-4D-05	Emergency Response
1-CORE-1A-03	Sanitation	1-CORE-4D-07	Confidentiality
1-CORE-1A-05	Water Supply	1-CORE-4D-08	Informed Consent
1-CORE-1C-01	Emergencies	1-CORE-4D-09	Involuntary Administration
1-CORE-1C-02	Emergencies	1-CORE-4D-10	Research
1-CORE-1C-03	Emergencies	1-CORE-4D-11	Use of Restraints
1-CORE-1C-04	Fire Safety	1-CORE-4D-16	Sexual Assault
1-CORE-1C-05	Fire Safety	1-CORE-4D-17	Inmate Death/Health Care Internal Review and Quality Assurance
1-CORE-1C-06	Fire Safety		
1-CORE-1C-07	Fire Safety		
1-CORE-2A-22	Special Management Inmates	1-CORE-5C-05	Work and Correctional Industries
1-CORE-2B-01	Use of Force		
1-CORE-2B-06	Weapons	1-CORE-6A-06	Protection from Abuse
1-CORE-2D-01	Key, Tool, and Utensil Control	1-CORE-7B-01	Training and Staff Development
1-CORE-4A-01	Dietary Allowances		
1-CORE-4A-03	Food Service Facilities		
1-CORE-4A-04	Health Protection		
1-CORE-4A-05	Health Protection		
1-CORE-4C-01	Access to Care/Clinical Services		
1-CORE-4C-03	Emergency Services		
1-CORE-4C-05	Pregnancy Management		
1-CORE-4C-06	Communicable Disease and Infection Control Program		
1-CORE-4C-07	Chronic Care		
1-CORE-4C-09	Health Screens		
1-CORE-4C-10	Health Screens		
1-CORE-4C-11	Health Appraisal		
1-CORE-4C-12	Mental Health Program		
1-CORE-4C-13	Suicide Prevention and Intervention		
1-CORE-4C-14	Detoxification		
1-CORE-4C-15	Pharmaceuticals		
1-CORE-4D-01	Health Authority		
1-CORE-4D-03	Provision of Treatment		

The Fundamentals of Performance-Based Standards

ACA's performance-based standards have several elements:

- **Goal Statement** (one for each functional area)
- **Performance Standards** (as many as are needed to achieve the goal)
- **Outcome Measures** for each performance standard
- **Expected Practices** for each standard
- **Protocols** (corresponding to each standard)
- **Process Indicators**

These elements are defined and described in Table 2.

Table 2: Definitions of Terms for Performance-Based Standards

Element	Definition
Goal Statement	General statement of what is sought within the functional area
Standard	A statement that clearly defines a required or essential *condition* to be achieved and maintained. A performance standard describes a "state of being," a condition, and does not describe the activities or practices that might be necessary to achieve compliance. Performance standards reflect the program's overall mission and purpose.
Outcome Measure	** Note: Outcome Measures are currently being developed for the Core Jail Standards* Measurable events, occurrences, conditions, behaviors or attitudes that demonstrate the extent to which the condition described in the performance standard has been achieved. Outcome measures describe the consequences of the program's activities, rather than describing the activities themselves. Outcome measures can be compared over time to indicate changes in the conditions that are sought. Outcome measure data are collected continuously but usually are analyzed periodically.
Expected Practice (s)	Actions and activities that, if implemented properly (according to protocols), will produce the desired outcome. What we *think* is necessary to achieve and maintain compliance with the standard--but not necessarily the *only* way to do so. These are activities that represent the current experience of the field, but that are not necessarily supported by research. As the field learns and evolves, so will practices.
Protocol(s)	Written instructions that guide implementation of expected practices, such as: policies/procedures, post orders, training curriculum, formats to be used such as logs and forms, offender handbooks, diagrams such as fire exit plans, internal inspection forms.
Process Indicators	Documentation and other evidence that can be examined periodically and continuously to determine that practices are being implemented properly. These "tracks" or "footprints" allow supervisory and management staff to monitor ongoing operations.

Table 3 attempts to describe the functional relationships among the elements.

Table 3: Functional Relationship Among Elements of Performance-Based Standards

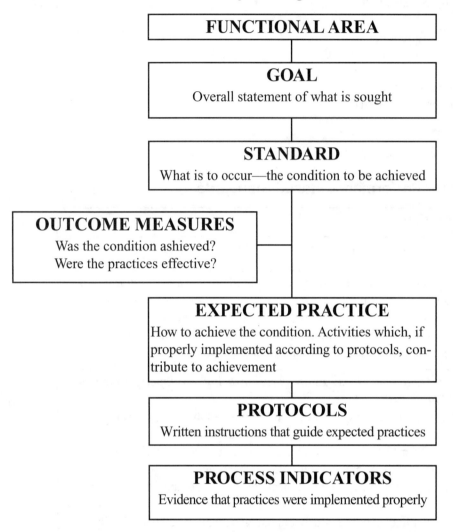

Each element is described and discussed in more detail in the following narrative.

GOAL STATEMENT

Perhaps the least-appreciated element of the template, the goal statement, attempts to establish an overall purpose for the standards in the functional area.

PERFORMANCE STANDARD

A performance standard is a statement that clearly defines a required or essential condition to be achieved and maintained. A performance standard describes a "state of being," a condition, and does not describe the activities or practices that might be necessary to achieve compliance. Performance standards reflect the program's overall mission and purpose and contribute to the realization of the goal that has been articulated.

The drafters of the new standards found it difficult to articulate clear and concise standards. The closer a draft standard came to meeting the definition of a performance-based standard, the simpler it seemed to appear. It is not unusual for someone to read a performance-based standard and think "Well, duh."

In drafting the new performance-based standards, the committee was constantly fighting the urge to describe an activity rather than to identify the overarching purpose for the activity. During many of the working group meetings, it was common for a proposed standard to be met with the response "Why?" While often frustrating, by continuing to ask the "why" question, the drafters were able to identify the basic statements of conditions that must be defined through performance standards.

Because performance standards are so fundamental and basic, it is less likely that they will require frequent revision. However, as the field continues to learn from experience, we predict and even hope that the expected practices that are prescribed to achieve compliance with standards will continue to evolve.

OUTCOME MEASURES

* Note: Outcome Measures are currently being developed for the Core Jail Standards

Outcome measures are quantifiable (measurable) events, occurrences, conditions, behaviors, or attitudes that demonstrate the extent to which the condition described in the corresponding performance standard has been achieved. Outcome measures describe the consequences of the organization's activities, rather than describing the activities themselves.

Because outcome measures are quantifiable, they can be compared over time to indicate changes in the conditions that are sought. Outcome-measure data are collected continuously but are usually analyzed periodically. The first time an outcome is measured, a point of reference is established. By comparing the next measurement (weeks or months later), progress, or a lack of progress, can be identified toward the desired outcome.

Outcome measures are distinct from a program's activities. For example, counting the number of vaccinations given to inmates is not an outcome measure (it is a performance indicator), but measuring the incidence of disease in the inmate population is an outcome measure. Also, the number of inmates who were provided with substance-abuse treatment would be a process indicator; the number of inmates who pass drug-screening tests would be an outcome measure. Outcome measures should be expressed as a ratio whenever possible—such as number of walk-aways per offender bed-days.

Most performance standards have several outcome measures that may be used to determine if the condition described in the standard has been achieved. Conversely, a single outcome measure might be used to ascertain compliance for more than one standard. Outcome measures look at the bigger picture by asking, "what actually happened?"

EXPECTED PRACTICES

Expected practices are actions and activities that, if implemented properly (according to protocols), will produce the desired outcome—achievement of the condition described in the standard.

Expected practices represent what the practitioners believe is necessary to achieve and maintain compliance with the standard—but may not be the only way to achieve compliance. These are activities that represent the best thinking of the field and are supported by experience but are not usually founded on research. As conditions change and experience is gained, practices are expected to evolve. It is arguable that expected practices should be changed over time to reflect the growing body of knowledge and experience. On the other hand, it is likely that much less change will be seen with the overarching performance standards, which are more basic and fundamental.

PROTOCOLS

Protocols are written instructions that guide implementation of expected practices, such as:

- Policies/procedures
- Post orders
- Training curriculum
- Formats to be used such as logs and forms
- Diagrams such as fire-exit plans
- Internal inspection forms

Protocols provide a map to guide the proper implementation of expected practices. Protocols describe, usually in great detail, how to implement activities that are described in expected practices.

PROCESS INDICATORS

Process indicators can be used frequently—even continuously—to monitor activities and practices. Yet, process indicators are not an "end" in and of themselves—they just tell if the expected practices are being implemented.

More about Outcome Measures and Process Indicators

Understanding the difference between outcome measures and process indicators can be difficult. *Process indicators* relate directly to expected practices. Process indicators tell if you are doing what you set out to do. Several expected practices address the provision of services to inmates. Process indicators can establish that various activities actually were delivered. However, it is the outcome measures that determine whether offenders were affected positively.

Most of the process indicators referenced in this manual refer to written documentation that can be consulted "after the fact." In addition to these "footprints" that are left by an organization, implementation of expected practices may be confirmed during an on-site inspection or audit by such activities as:

- Observations
- Interviews (with staff, volunteers, offenders, and others)

These additional activities (observations and interview) are also a central part of ACA's certification process, including much of the work that is conducted on-site during audits. Certification participants will also recognize many of the protocols described in this manual as the "primary documentation" required by ACA as part of the certification process. Similarly, the Commission on Accreditation for Corrections currently uses many of the process indicators as "secondary documentation" for corrections.

Note that the observations and interview activities usually are suggested only when other methods are not possible. Observing, interviewing, and measuring rely on an on-site "single point in time" activity, while the other methods enable the users to examine practices randomly, over a longer period of time.

Outcome measures look at the "bottom line." Were expected practices properly implemented? Was the desired condition or state of being described in the performance standard achieved? Outcome measures may be expressed in three basic ways:

- As <u>rates</u> (the frequency of an occurrence over time, such as the number of serious fires/year)

- As <u>ratios</u> (comparing two numbers as a fraction or decimal, such as the number of inmates diagnosed with hepatitis divided by the average daily population)

- As <u>proportions</u> (the relation of a part to the whole, such as the number of inmate grievances found in favor of the inmate divided by the total number of grievances filed). A percentage is a proportion multiplied by 100.

Rarely does an outcome measure call for simply counting an event or occurrence. Outcome measures should include a numerator and a denominator if they are to be useful as a management tool.

Whenever possible, the drafters tried to use denominators that reflect the volume of activity. Therefore, it is preferable to divide by the average daily population rather than simply counting the number of events per month. The "Average Daily Inmate Population for the Past Twelve Months" is used whenever appropriate. In a few instances, other denominators have been used. What do the numbers mean after the math is done? They provide a starting point for analyzing and assessing the organization.

The first time outcome measures are generated, they will not mean much, but their value grows every time they are used. The second time outcomes are measured, current outcomes can be compared to those that were measured in the past. In this way, outcome measures become a valuable management tool. Over time, the series of outcome measures that are calculated can provide invaluable insight into various aspects of the operation. Sometimes they will provide important "red flags" that identify troubling trends.

1. Safety

GOAL: Provide a safe environment for the community, staff, volunteers, contractors, and inmates.

PERFORMANCE STANDARD: Protection from Injury and Illness

1A. **The community, staff, volunteers, contractors, and inmates are protected from injury and illness in the workplace.**

EXPECTED PRACTICES

Sanitation Inspections

1-CORE-1A-01 (Mandatory)
(Ref. 4-ALDF-1A-01)   **The facility complies with all applicable laws and regulations of the governing jurisdiction. The following inspections are implemented:**

- weekly sanitation inspections of all facility areas by a qualified departmental staff member
- comprehensive and thorough monthly inspections by a safety/sanitation specialist
- at least annual inspections by qualified persons

Comment: None.

Protocols: Written policy and procedure. Sanitation and safety inspection checklists. Laws and regulations.
Process Indicators: Completed inspection checklists and reports. Documentation of corrective action. Inspection reports.

Disposal of Material

1-CORE-1A 02 (Mandatory)
(Ref. 4-ALDF-1A-02)   **Disposal of liquid, solid, and hazardous material complies with applicable government regulations.**

Comment: None.

Protocols: Written policy and procedure. Written plan. Internal health/sanitation inspection checklists that include solid waste issues.
Process Indicators: Plan that has been approved by regulatory agency. Trash disposal contract. Completed inspection reports/forms, including documentation that identified deficiencies were corrected. Observation.

Vermin and Pests

1-CORE-1A-03 (Mandatory)
(Ref. 4-ALDF-1A-03)   **Vermin and pests are controlled.**

Comment: None.

Protocols: Written policy and procedure. Control plan.
Process Indicators: Pest control contracts. Maintenance agreements. Trash disposal contracts. Inspection reports, including documentation that identified deficiencies were corrected.

Housekeeping

1-CORE-1A-04
(Ref. 4-ALDF-1A-04)   **The facility is clean and in good repair.**

Comment: None.

Protocols: Written policy and procedure. Housekeeping plan. Maintenance plan. Inspection forms. Inmate handbook (describing inmate responsibilities).
Process Indicators: Inspection reports, completed forms, including documentation that identified deficiencies were corrected.

Water Supply

1-CORE-1A-05 (Mandatory)
(Ref. 4-ALDF-1A-07)   **The facility's potable water source and supply, whether owned and operated by a public water department or the facility, is certified at least annually by an independent, outside source to be in compliance with jurisdictional laws and regulations.**

Comment: None.

Protocols: Written policy and procedure.
Process Indicators: Documentation of approval by outside source. Documentation of credentials of person/agency providing approval.

Single-Occupancy Cells (Size)

1-CORE-1A-06 (Existing, Renovation, Addition, New Construction)
(Ref. 4-ALDF-1A-09) **Single cells provide at least 35 square feet of unencumbered space. At least 70 square feet of total floor space is provided when the occupant is confined for more than ten hours per day.**

Comment: "Unencumbered space" is usable space that is not encumbered by furnishings or fixtures. At least one dimension of the unencumbered space is no less than seven feet. In determining the unencumbered space, the total square footage is obtained and the square footage of the fixtures is subtracted. All fixtures must be in operational position for these calculations.

Protocols: Written policy and procedure. Facility plans/specifications.
Process Indicators: Measurement. Observation.

Multiple-Occupancy Rooms/Cells (Size)

1-CORE-1A-07 (Existing, Renovation, Addition, New Construction)
(Ref. 4-ALDF-1A-10) **Multiple-occupancy rooms/cells house between two and sixty-four occupants and provide 25 square feet of unencumbered space per occupant. When confinement exceeds ten hours per day, at least 35 square feet of unencumbered space is provided for each occupant**

Comment: "Unencumbered space" is usable space that is not encumbered by furnishings or fixtures. At least one dimension of the unencumbered space is no less than seven feet. In determining the unencumbered space, the total square footage is obtained and the square footage of the fixtures is subtracted. All fixtures must be in operational position for these calculations.

Protocols: Written policy and procedure. Facility plans/specifications.
Process Indicators: Measurement. Observation.

Dayrooms (Size)

1-CORE-1A-08 (Existing, Renovation, Addition, New Construction)
(Ref. 4-ALDF-1A-12) **Dayrooms with space for varied inmate activities are situated immediately adjacent to inmate sleeping areas. Dayrooms provide a minimum of 35 square feet of space per inmate (exclusive of lavatories, showers, and toilets) for the maximum number of inmates who use the dayroom at one time. No dayroom encompasses less than 100 square feet of space, exclusive of lavatories, showers, and toilets.**

Comment: None.

Protocols: Written policy and procedure. Facility plans/specifications.
Process Indicators: Measurement. Observation. Interviews (staff, inmates). Housing and classification records/logs.

Environmental Conditions/Lighting

1-CORE-1A-09
(Ref. 4-ALDF-1A-14, 1A-15)   **All inmate rooms/cells provide the occupants with access to natural light. Lighting throughout the facility is sufficient for the tasks performed.**

Comment: None.

Protocols: Written policy and procedure. Facility plans/specifications.
Process Indicators: Documentation from a qualified source. Measurement. Observation. Maintenance and repair records. Inmate and staff interviews.

Ventilation

1-CORE-1A-10
(Ref. 4-ALDF-1A-19, 1A-20)   **A ventilation system supplies at least 15 cubic feet per minute of circulated air per occupant, with a minimum of five cubic feet per minute of outside air. Toilet rooms and cells with toilets have no less than four air changes per hour unless state or local codes require a different number of air changes. Air quantities are documented by a qualified independent source and are checked not less than once per accreditation cycle. Temperatures are mechanically raised or lowered to acceptable comfort levels.**

Comment: Accreditation cycle is defined as within the past three years.

Protocols: Written policy and procedure. Facility plans/specifications.
Process Indicators: Measurement. Observation. Inmate and staff interviews. Facility logs and records. Maintenance and repair records. Report from independent source.

Smoking

1-CORE-1A-11
(Ref. 4-ALDF-1A-21)   **Non-smoking inmates are not exposed to secondhand smoke.**

Comment: Research confirms the adverse health effects of environmental tobacco smoke (secondhand smoke).

Protocols: Written policy and procedure. Inmate handbook, rules.
Process Indicators: Observation. Staff and inmate interviews. Facility logs and records.

PERFORMANCE STANDARD: Vehicle Safety

1B. Vehicles are maintained and operated in a manner that prevents harm to the community, staff, contractors, volunteers, and inmates.

EXPECTED PRACTICES

Vehicles/Inmate Transport

1-CORE-1B-01
(Ref. 4-ALDF-1B-03,
1B-04, 1B-06)

Transportation of inmates outside the facility, and security of facility vehicles are governed by policy and procedure. Staff involved with transportation of inmates are informed of all policies and procedures. Annual safety inspections are conducted on all vehicles used by the facility. Repairs are completed immediately. Vehicles are not used until repairs are completed.

Comment: None.

Protocols: Written policy/procedure. Vehicle log format. Maintenance record format. Staff training curriculum.
Process Indicators: Inspection reports. Completed vehicle logs. Maintenance records and receipts. Reports of vehicle problems/requests for repair or maintenance. Credentials of inspector. Documentation of completed repairs. Documentation of staff training and qualifications. Transport logs. Staff and inmate interviews.

PERFORMANCE STANDARD Emergency Preparedness/Response

1C. The number and severity of emergencies are minimized. When emergencies occur, the response minimizes the severity.

Definition: An emergency is any event that results in the suspension or disruption of normal facility operations.

EXPECTED PRACTICES

Emergency Plan

1-CORE-1C-01 (Mandatory)
(Ref. 4-ALDF-1C-01, 1C-05, 1C-06)

There is a plan that guides the facility response to emergencies. All facility personnel are trained annually in the implementation of the emergency plan. The emergency plan should include procedures to be followed in situations that threaten facility security. Such situations may include but are not limited to: riots/disturbances, hunger strikes, escapes, taking of hostages, and staff work stoppage.

Comment: None.

Protocols: Written policy and procedure. Emergency plans. Training curriculum. Distribution list for plan.
Process Indicators: Training records. Facility logs. Staff interviews and training records. Distribution records. Documentation of annual review. Documentation of staff receipt of, and training on, the plan.

Evacuation Plan

1-CORE-1C-02 (Mandatory)
(Ref. 4-ALDF-1C-02)

An evacuation plan is used in the event of fire or major emergency. The plan is approved by an independent outside inspector trained in the application of national fire safety codes and is reviewed annually, updated if necessary, and reissued to the local fire jurisdiction.

Comment: None.

Protocols: Written policy and procedure. Facility plans/specifications. Evacuation plan.
Process Indicators: Documentation of approval of plan. Documentation of annual review. Observation. Documentation of drills. Staff and inmate interviews.

Immediate Release of Inmates

1-CORE-1C-03 (Mandatory)
(Ref. 4-ALDF-1C-03, 1C-04) **There is a means for the immediate release of inmates from locked areas in case of emergency, and there are provisions for a backup system. The facility has exits that are properly positioned, are clear from obstruction, and are distinctly and permanently marked to ensure the timely evacuation of inmates and staff in the event of fire or other emergency. All housing areas and places of assembly for fifty or more persons have two exits.**

Comment: None.

Protocols: Written policy and procedure. Facility plans/specifications. Emergency release plan.
Process Indicators: Observation. Staff interviews. Facility records/logs.

Fire Safety

Code Conformance

1-CORE-1C-04 (Mandatory)
(Ref. 4-ALDF-1C-07) **The facility conforms to applicable federal, state, and/or local fire safety codes.**

Comment: None.

Protocols: Written policy and procedure. Facility plans/specifications. Fire regulations and codes. Internal inspection forms. Detention and alarm system testing schedule.
Process Indicators: Documentation of compliance. Reports/inspections from external agencies. Internal inspection results and reports. Documentation of fire alarm and detection system maintenance and testing. Observation.

Fire Prevention Regulations

1-CORE-1C-05 (Mandatory)

(Ref. 4-ALDF-1C-08, 1C-09)

The facility's fire prevention regulations and practices ensure the safety of staff, contractors, inmates, and visitors. There is a comprehensive and thorough monthly inspection of the facility by a qualified fire and safety officer for compliance with safety and fire prevention standards. There is an annual inspection by local or state fire officials or other qualified persons.

Comment: None.

Protocols: Written policy and procedure. Fire prevention regulations. Internal inspection forms. Facility plans/specifications. Training curricula. Equipment testing schedule.

Process Indicators: Maintenance and testing records. Observation. Facility logs. Staff training records. Reports describing fire events that occurred. Staff interviews. Documentation of qualifications of fire and safety officer. Inspection reports and documentation of action taken to address identified deficiencies. Local and/or state inspection reports.

Facility Furnishings

1-CORE-1C-06 (Mandatory)

(Ref. 4-ALDF-1C-10)

Facility furnishings meet fire-safety-performance requirements.

Comment: Facility furnishings include draperies, curtains, furniture, mattresses and bedding, upholstered or cushioned furniture, wastebaskets, decorations, and similar materials that can burn. Furnishings, mattresses, cushions, or other items of foamed plastics or foamed rubber (for example, polyurethane, polystyrene) can pose a severe hazard due to high smoke production, rapid burning once ignited, and high heat release. Such materials should be subjected to careful fire-safety evaluation before purchase or use. All polyurethane should be removed from living areas unless its use is approved in writing by the fire authority having jurisdiction. The fire authority should consider the flammability and toxicity characteristics of the products being evaluated. "Furnishings" applies to all living quarters. This expected practice requires that specifications be known, if available, at the time of selection. There are no expected practices mandating knowledge of fire-performance characteristics of furnishings in the facility prior to implementation of the policy relating to this expected practice.

Protocols: Written policy and procedure. Facility plans/specifications.

Process Indicators: Specifications for all furnishings. Records of approval by external authority.

Flammable, Toxic, and Caustic Materials

1-CORE-1C-07 (Mandatory)
4-ALDF-1C-11	**Flammable, toxic, and caustic materials are controlled and used safely.**

Comment: None.

Protocols: Written policy and procedure. Facility plans/specifications. Staff training curriculum. Inmate training curriculum. Inmate handbook/rules. Internal inspection forms.
Process Indicators: Staff training records. Inmate training records. Internal inspection results. Documentation of incidents that involved flammable, toxic, or caustic materials.

Emergency Power and Communication

Essential Lighting and Life-Sustaining Functions

1-CORE-1C-08
(Ref. 4-ALDF-1C-12)	**Essential lighting and life-sustaining functions are maintained inside the facility or by the community in an emergency.**

Comment: None.

Protocols: Written policy and procedure. Facility plans/specifications.
Process Indicators: Observation. Facility records and logs.

Equipment is in Working Order

1-CORE-1C-09
(Ref. 4-ALDF-1C-14)	**All equipment is in working order. Safety and security equipment is repaired or replaced immediately. Use of padlocks for security locks on cell or inmate housing doors is prohibited.**

Comment: None.

Protocols: Written policy and procedure. Job descriptions. Emergency repair plan.
Process Indicators: Facility records/logs. Personnel records.

2. Security

GOAL: Protect the community, staff, contractors, volunteers, and inmates from harm.

PERFORMANCE STANDARD: Protection from Harm

2A. The community, staff, contractors, volunteers, and inmates are protected from harm. Events that pose a risk of harm are prevented. The number and severity of events are minimized.

EXPECTED PRACTICES

Control

1-CORE-2A-01
(Ref. 4-ALDF-2A-01)

The facility's security, life safety, and communications systems are monitored continuously from a secure location.

Comment: None.

Protocols: Written policy and procedure. Facility plans/specifications. Staff schedules.
Process Indicators: Facility records and logs. Observation. Maintenance records.

Correctional Officers' Posts

1-CORE-2A-02
(Ref. 4-ALDF-2A-03, 2A-04)

Correctional officers' posts are located adjacent to inmate living areas to permit officers to see or hear and respond promptly to emergency situations. There are written orders for every correctional officer's post.

Comment: None.

Protocols: Written policy and procedure. Facility plans/specifications. Post orders. Acknowledgment form.
Process Indicators: Observation. Staff and inmate interviews. Documentation of staff receipt of post orders. Documentation of annual review and updating.

Personal Contact Between Staff and Inmates

1-CORE-2A-03
(Ref. 4-ALDF-2A-05, 2A-06)

Personal contact and interaction between staff and inmates is required. The facility administrator or designee visits the facility's living and activity areas at least weekly.

Comment: None.

Protocols: Written policy and procedure. Facility plans/specifications. Schedule.
Process Indicators: Observation. Facility logs. Staff and inmate interviews.

Secure Perimeter

1-CORE-2A-04
(Ref. 4-ALDF-2A-07)

The facility perimeter ensures inmates are secured and that access by the general public is denied without proper authorization.

Comment: None.

Protocols: Written policy and procedure. Facility plans/specifications.
Process Indicators: Observation. Facility records and logs.

Female Inmate and Female Staff

1-CORE-2A-05
(Ref. 4-ALDF-2A-08)

When a female inmate is housed in a facility, at least one female staff member is on duty at all times.

Comment: None.

Protocols: Written policy and procedure. Staffing plans.
Process Indicators: Records of staff deployment. Facility logs.

No Inmate Control Over Others

1-CORE-2A-06
(Ref. 4-ALDF-2A-09)

No inmate or group of inmates is given control, or allowed to exert authority, over other inmates.

Comment: None.

Protocols: Written policy and procedure.
Process Indicators: Observation. Staff and inmate interviews.

Inmate Movement under Staff Control

1-CORE-2A-07
(Ref. 4-ALDF-2A-10)

All inmate movement from one area to another is controlled by staff.

Comment: None.

Protocols: Written policy and procedure. Facility plans/specifications. Staffing plans.
Process Indicators: Observation.

Staff Log

1-CORE-2A-08
(Ref. 4-ALDF-2A-11)

Correctional staff maintain a permanent log and prepare shift reports that record routine information, emergency situations, and unusual incidents.

Comment: Permanent logs may be recorded electronically.

Protocols: Written policy and procedure. Record keeping forms and formats.
Process Indicators: Completed logs and other records. Documentation of emergency situations and unusual incidents.

Staffing

Sufficient Staff

1-CORE-2A-09
(Ref. 4-ALDF-2A-14)

Sufficient staff, including a designated supervisor, are provided at all times to perform functions relating to the security, custody, and supervision of inmates and, as needed, to operate the facility in conformance with the standards.

Comment: None.

Protocols: Written policy and procedure. Staffing analysis process and plan. Staff deployment plans and schedules.
Process Indicators: Documentation of annual review of staffing analysis and plan. Records of actual staff deployment. Facility logs.

Inmate Counts

Inmate Population Management System

1-CORE-2A-10
(Ref. 4-ALDF-2A-16)

There is an inmate-population-management process that includes records on the admission, processing, and release of inmates.

Comment: None.

Protocols: Written policy and procedure. Accounting system. Forms. Report formats.
Process Indicators: Completed forms. Reports. Staff interviews.

Counts

1-CORE-2A-11
(Ref. 4-ALDF-
2A-17)
The facility has a system for physically counting inmates. At least one formal count is conducted for each shift, with no less than three counts daily.

Comment: Electronic means should not be substituted for direct staff observation.

Protocols: Written policy and procedure. Accounting system. Forms. Identification forms/formats.
Process Indicators: Completed forms. Facility records and logs. Documentation of inmate accounting activities. Staff interviews.

Facility Design

1-CORE-2A-12 (Renovation, Addition, New construction only).
(Ref. 4-ALDF-
2A-18)
Physical plant design facilitates continuous personal contact and interaction between staff and inmates in housing units. All living areas are constructed to facilitate continuous staff observation, excluding electronic surveillance, of cell or detention room fronts and areas such as dayrooms and recreation spaces.

Comment: None.

Protocols: Written policy and procedure. Facility plans/specifications.
Process Indicators: Observation. Staff and inmate interviews.

Reception

Legal Commitment and Medical Review

1-CORE-2A-13
(Ref. 4-ALDF-
2A-19)
Prior to accepting custody of an inmate, staff determine that the inmate is legally committed to the facility, and that the inmate is not in need of immediate medical attention.

Comment: None.

Protocols: Written policy and procedure. Admission forms.
Process Indicators: Completed admissions forms. Facility logs. Observation.

Admissions

1-CORE-2A-14
(Ref. 4-ALDF-2A-20, 2A-21, 2A-23)

Admission processes for a newly admitted inmate include, but are not limited to:

- **searching of the inmate and personal property**
- **inventorying and providing secure storage of personal property**
- **providing an itemized receipt of personal property**
- **recording of basic personal data**
- **performing a criminal history check**
- **photographing and fingerprinting, as required**
- **medical, dental, and mental health screening**
- **suicide screening**
- **separating from the general population**

Comment: None.

Protocols: Written policy and procedure. Intake and admission forms. Screening forms. Staff training curriculum. Inventory form. Receipt form.
Process Indicators: Observations. Staff and inmate interview. Intake records/files. Intake and admission records. Completed inventory forms and receipts.

Orientation

1-CORE-2A-15
(Ref. 4-ALDF-2A-27)

Prior to being placed in the general population, each inmate is provided with an orientation that includes facility rules and regulations, including access to medical care. Facility rules and regulations are available during their confinement. The written materials are translated into those languages spoken by a significant number of inmates.

Comment: None.

Protocols: Written policy and procedure. Orientation information and process. Inmate handbook.
Process Indicators: Observation. Intake records. Inmate interviews.

Classification and Separation

Objective Classification System

1-CORE-2A-16
(Ref. 4-ALDF-
2A-30, 2A-31)

An objective classification system is used to separate inmates into groups to reduce the probability of assault and disruptive behavior. All inmates are classified using an objective classification process that at a minimum:

- **Identifies the appropriate level of custody for each inmate**
- **Identifies appropriate housing assignment**
- **Identifies the inmate's interest and eligibility to participate in available programs**

There is a process for review and appeal of classification decisions.

Comment: None.

Protocols: Written policy and procedure. Classification forms and formats. Methodology for validating process. Process for periodic review and appeal. Inmate handbook. Inmate orientation materials.
Process Indicators: Classification records. Documentation of verification of the process. Documentation of periodic review and appeal. Inmate interviews.

Separation in Classification

1-CORE-2A-17
(Ref. 4-ALDF-
2A-32, 2A-33)

Inmate management and housing assignment considers age, gender, legal status, custody needs, special problems and needs, and behavior. Male and female inmates are housed in separate rooms/cells. Inmates are separated according to existing laws and regulations and/or consistent with the facility's classification plan.

Comment: None.

Protocols: Written policy and procedure. Housing assignment process and forms. Facility plans/specifications. Applicable statutes and regulations. Classification plan.
Process Indicators: Inmate housing records. Observation. Staff and inmate interviews. Inmate classification records. Observation.

Single-Occupancy Cells

1-CORE-2A-18
(Ref. 4-ALDF-
2A-34)

Inmates not suitable for housing in multiple occupancy cells are housed in single occupancy cells.

Comment: None.

Protocols: Written policy and procedure. Facility plans/specifications.
Process Indicators: Observation. Interviews (staff, inmates.) Housing and classification records/logs.

Youthful Offenders

Prohibition on Youthful Offenders

1-CORE-2A-19
(Ref. 4-ALDF-2A-37)

Confinement of juveniles under the age of eighteen is prohibited unless a court finds that it is in the best interest of justice and public safety that a juvenile awaiting trial or other legal process be treated as an adult for the purposes of prosecution, or unless convicted as an adult and required by statute to be confined in an adult facility.

Comment: None.

Protocols: Written policy and procedure.
Process Indicators: Observation. Interviews (staff, inmates). Admission and housing.

Plan for Youthful Offenders

1-CORE-2A-20
(Ref. 4-ALDF-2A-38, 2A-39, 2A-40, 2A-43)

If juveniles are committed to the facility, a plan is in place to provide for the following:

- **supervision and programming needs of the juveniles to ensure their safety, security, and education**
- **classification and housing plans**
- **appropriately trained staff**

Comment: American Correctional Association policy prohibits confinement of youthful offenders in an adult facility; however, where the laws of the jurisdiction require such confinement, the provisions of the standard must be met.

Protocols: Written policy and procedure. Youthful offender classification plan. Facility plans/specifications. Staff training curriculum. Job description. Staffing plan.
Process Indicators: Facility logs and records. Inmate records. Staff interviews. Documentation of decisions and actions with individual youthful offenders. Classification records. Staff credentials. Staff training records. Staff deployment records.

Special Management Inmates

Segregation for Protection

1-CORE-2A-21
(Ref. 4-ALDF-
2A-44)
The facility administrator or designee can order immediate segregation when it is necessary to protect an inmate or others. The action is reviewed within 72 hours by the appropriate authority.

Comment: None.

Protocols: Written policy and procedure.
Process Indicators: Documentation of review within 72 hours. Facility records. Inmate records.

Health Care

1-CORE-2A-22 (Mandatory)
(Ref. 4-ALDF-
2A-45)
When an inmate is transferred to segregation, health care personnel are informed immediately and provide assessment and review, as indicated by the protocols established by the health authority.

Comment: Health care provider's visits are intended to be screening rounds and are not meant to be clinical encounters. The visit ensures that inmates have access to the health care system. The health care provider determines the appropriate setting for further medical attention or examination and may request an inmate's removal from a cell or housing area to a clinical environment.

Protocols: Written policy and procedure.
Process Indicators: Health records. Segregation logs. Duty assignment roster for health care providers. Observation. Interviews.

Conditions of Segregation

1-CORE-2A-23
(Ref. 4-ALDF-
2A-51)
Segregation housing units provide living conditions that approximate those of the general inmate population. All exceptions are clearly documented. Segregation cells/rooms permit the inmates assigned to them to be able to converse with and be observed by staff members.

Comment: None.

Protocols: Written policy and procedure. Facility plans/specifications.
Process Indicators: Observation. Measurement. Inmate interviews.

Observation of Special Management Inmates

1-CORE-2A-24
**(Ref. 4-ALDF-
2A-52)**

All special management inmates are personally observed by a correctional officer at least every 30 minutes on an irregular schedule. Inmates who are violent or mentally disordered or who demonstrate unusual or bizarre behavior are assessed by medical personnel, who determine the level of supervision needed.

Comment: None.

Protocols: Written policy and procedure. Staffing plan. Log format.
Process Indicators: Facility records and logs. Documentation of cell checks.

PERFORMANCE STANDARD: Use of Physical Force

2B. Physical force is used only in instances of self-protection, protection of the inmate or others, prevention of property damage, or prevention of escape.

EXPECTED PRACTICES

Use of Force

Restrictions on Use of Force

1-CORE-2B-01 (Mandatory)
(Ref. 4-ALDF-2B-01)

The use of physical force is restricted to instances of justifiable self-defense, protection of others, protection of property, and prevention of escapes, and then only as a last resort and in accordance with appropriate statutory authority. In no event is physical force used as punishment.

Comment: None.

Protocols: Written policy and procedure. Staff training curriculum.
Process Indicators: Facility records and logs. Incident reports. Training records.

Restraints

Restraint Devices

1-CORE-2B-02
(Ref. 4-ALDF-2B-02)

Restraint devices are never applied as punishment. There are defined circumstances under which supervisory approval is needed prior to application.

Comment: Restraint devices should be used only to prevent self-injury, injury to others, or property damage. Restraints are not applied for more time than is necessary.

Protocols: Written policy and procedure.
Process Indicators: Documentation of supervisory approval. Staff interviews.

Four/Five Point Restraints

1-CORE-2B-03 (Mandatory)
(Ref. 4-ALDF-
2B-03)

Four/five point restraints are used only in extreme instances and only when other types of restraints have proven ineffective. Advance approval is secured from the facility administrator/designee before an inmate is placed in a four/five point restraint. Subsequently, the health authority or designee is notified to assess the inmate's medical and mental health condition, and to advise whether, on the basis of serious danger to self or others, the inmate should be in a medical/mental health unit for emergency involuntary treatment with sedation and/or other medical management, as appropriate. If the inmate is not transferred to a medical/ mental health unit and is restrained in a four/five point position, the following minimum procedures are followed:

- **continuous direct visual observation by staff prior to an assessment by the health authority or designee**
- **subsequent visual observation is made at least every 15 minutes**
- **restraint procedures are in accordance with guidelines approved by the designated health authority**
- **documentation of all decisions and actions**

Comment: A four/five point restraint secures an inmate's arms and legs (four point) and head (five point). Restraint guidelines include consideration of an individual's physical condition, such as body weight.

Protocols: Written policy and procedure. Forms.
Process Indicators: Observation. Facility records and logs. Inmate and staff interviews. Documentation of approval(s) and observation.

Weapons

Procedures for Weapons

1-CORE-2B-04
(Ref. 4-ALDF-
2B-04, 2B-05)

Procedures govern the availability, control, inventory, storage, and use of firearms, less lethal devices, and related security devices, and specify the level of authority required for their access and use. Chemical agents and electrical disablers are used only with the authorization of the facility administrator or designee. Access to storage areas is restricted to authorized persons and the storage space is located in an area separate and apart from inmate housing or activity areas.

Comment: None.

Protocols: Written policy and procedure. Authorization forms. Facility plans/ specifications.
Process Indicators: Facility logs and records. Completed authorization forms. Staff interviews.

Written Reports

1-CORE-2B-05
(Ref. 4-ALDF-2B-07)

Written reports are submitted to the facility administrator or designee no later than the conclusion of the tour of duty when any of the following occur:

- **discharge of a firearm or other weapon**
- **use of less lethal devices to control inmates**
- **use of force to control inmates**
- **inmate(s) remaining in restraints at the end of the shift**
- **routine and emergency distribution of security equipment**

Comment: None.

Protocols: Written policy and procedure. Report format.
Process Indicators: Completed reports. Facility records and logs.

Use of Firearms

1-CORE-2B-06 (Mandatory)
(Ref. 4-ALDF-2B-08)

The use of firearms complies with the following requirements:

- **weapons are subjected to stringent safety regulations and inspections**
- **a secure weapons locker is located outside the secure perimeter of the facility**
- **except in emergency situations, firearms and authorized weapons are permitted only in designated areas to which inmates have no access**
- **employees supervising inmates outside the facility perimeter follow procedures for the security of weapons**
- **employees are instructed to use deadly force only after other actions have been tried and found ineffective, unless the employee believes that a person's life is immediately threatened**
- **employees on duty use only firearms or other security equipment that have been approved by the facility administrator**
- **appropriate equipment is provided to facilitate safe unloading and loading of firearms**

Comment: None.

Protocols: Written policy and procedure. Facility plans/specifications. Staff training curriculum.
Process Indicators: Training records. Observation. Staff and inmate interviews.

PERFORMANCE STANDARD: Contraband/Searches

2C. Contraband is minimized. It is detected when present in the facility.

EXPECTED PRACTICES

Searches

Procedures for Searches

**1-CORE-2C-01
(Ref. 4-ALDF-
2C-01)**

Procedures guide searches of facilities and inmates to control contraband

Comment: None.

Protocols: Written policy and procedure. Search procedures.
Process Indicators: Observation. Facility records and logs. Inmate and staff interviews.

Arrestee Strip Search

**1-CORE-2C-02
(Ref. 4-ALDF-
2C-03)**

A strip search of an arrestee at intake is only conducted when there is reasonable belief or suspicion that he/she may be in possession of an item of contraband. The least-invasive form of search is conducted.

Comment: For arrestees, generally the least-invasive form of search should be conducted.

Protocols: Written policy and procedure. Search procedures.
Process Indicators: Observation. Facility records and logs. Inmate and staff interviews.

Inmate Strip Search

**1-CORE-2C-03
(Ref. 4-ALDF-
2C-04)**

A strip search of a general population inmate is only conducted when there is reasonable belief that the inmate may be in possession of an item of contraband or when the inmate leaves the confines of the facility to go on an outside appointment or work detail and upon return from such outside appointment or work detail. The least-invasive form of search is conducted.

Comment: Reasonable belief may be based on: reliable information that the inmate possesses contraband; discovery of contraband in the inmate's living space; a serious incident in which the inmate was involved or where the inmate was present; refusal to be searched; contact with the public or exposure to public areas; exposure to contact visits; or return to custody from community status.

Protocols: Written policy and procedure. Search procedures.
Process Indicators: Observation. Facility records and logs. Inmate and staff interviews.

Body Cavity Search

1-CORE-2C-04
(Ref. 4-ALDF-2C-05)   **Manual or instrument inspection of body cavities is conducted only when there is reasonable belief that the inmate is concealing contraband and when authorized by the facility administrator or designee. Health care personnel conduct the inspection in private.**

Comment: None.

Protocols: Written policy and procedure. Search procedures.
Process Indicators: Observation. Facility records and logs. Inmate and staff interviews. Credentials of personnel who conduct searches.

PERFORMANCE STANDARD: Access to Keys, Tools, Utensils

2D. Improper access to and use of keys, tools and utensils are minimized.

EXPECTED PRACTICES

Key, Tool, and Utensil Control

1-CORE-2D-01 (Mandatory)
(Ref. 4-ALDF-2D-01, 2D-02, 2D-03)   **Keys, tools, culinary equipment, and medical/dental instruments and supplies (syringes, needles and other sharps) are inventoried and use is controlled.**

Comment: None.

Protocols: Written policy and procedure. Key control plan. Inventory forms. Format for reports.
Process Indicators: Facility logs. Documentation of key control activities. Inventory logs and forms. Observation. Interviews.

3. Order

GOAL: Maintain an orderly environment with clear expectations of behavior and systems of accountability.

PERFORMANCE STANDARD: Inmate Discipline

3A. Inmates comply with rules and regulations.

EXPECTED PRACTICES

Rules and Discipline

1-CORE-3A-01 (Ref. 4-ALDF-3A-01, 3A-02, 2A-50)   **Disciplinary procedures governing inmate rule violations address the following:**

- **rules of inmate conduct that specify prohibited acts and appropriate sanctions for each prohibited act**
- **minor and major violations**
- **criminal offenses**
- **disciplinary reports**
- **pre-hearing actions/investigation**
- **pre-hearing detention**
- **placement of an inmate in disciplinary detention for a rule violation only after a hearing.**
- **maximum sanction for a rule violation is no more than sixty days**

Comment: The rules should prohibit only observed behavior that can be shown clearly to have a direct, adverse effect on an inmate or on facility order and security. Penalties should be proportionate to the importance of the rule and the severity of the violation.

Protocols: Written policy and procedure. Rules. Inmate handbook. Report formats. Sanctioning schedule.

Process Indicators: Documentation of annual review. Inmate records. Disciplinary records. Inmate and staff interviews. Documentation that sanctioning schedule has been communicated to inmates. Documentation of facility administrator review and approval.

4. Care

GOAL: Provide for the basic needs and personal care of inmates.

PERFORMANCE STANDARD: Food Service

4A. Food service provides a nutritionally balanced diet. Food service operations are hygienic and sanitary.

EXPECTED PRACTICES

Food

Dietary Allowances

1-CORE-4A-01 (Mandatory)
(Ref. 4-ALDF-4A-07)

The facility's dietary allowances are reviewed at least annually by a qualified nutritionist or dietician to ensure that they meet the nationally recommended dietary allowances for basic nutrition for appropriate age groups. Menu evaluations are conducted at least quarterly by food service supervisory staff to verify adherence to the established basic daily servings.

Comment: Copies of menu evaluations should be forwarded to the health authority.

Protocols: Written policy and procedure. Recommended dietary allowances.
Process Indicators: Annual reviews. Nutritionist or dietician qualifications. Documentation of at least annual review and quarterly menu evaluations. Interviews with staff.

Therapeutic or Special Diets

1-CORE-4A-02
(Ref. 4-ALDF-4A-09, 4A-10)

Therapeutic and/or special diets are provided as prescribed by appropriate clinicians or when religious beliefs require adherence to religious dietary laws.

Comment: Therapeutic diets are prepared and served to inmates according to the orders of the treating clinician or as directed by the responsible health authority official. Prescriptions for therapeutic diets should be specific and complete, furnished in writing to the food service manager, and rewritten quarterly. Therapeutic diets should be kept as simple as possible and should conform as closely as possible to the foods served other inmates. Pregnant women are only prescribed meals, if necessary.

Protocols: Written policy and procedures. Diet manual. Diet request form. Special diets.
Process Indicators: Health records. Diet records or forms. Observation. Interviews. Documentation of chaplain's approval. Diet manual.

Food Service Facilities

1-CORE-4A-03 (Mandatory)

(Ref. 4-ALDF-4A-11) **There is documentation by an independent, outside source that food service facilities and equipment meet established government health and safety codes. Corrective action is taken on any deficiencies.**

Comment: None.

Protocols: Written policy and procedure. Health and safety codes.
Process Indicators: Documentation of compliance with codes. Inspection reports, completed forms, including documentation that identified deficiencies were corrected.

Health Protection for Food Service

1-CORE-4A-04 (Mandatory)

(Ref. 4-ALDF-4A-13) **There is adequate health protection for all inmates and staff in the facility and for inmates and other persons working in food service. All persons involved in the preparation of the food receive a pre-assignment medical examination to ensure freedom from diarrhea, skin infections, and other illnesses transmissible by food or utensils.**

Comment: None.

Protocols: Written policy and procedure. Laws, statutes, and regulations.
Process Indicators: Inspection reports, completed forms, including documentation that identified deficiencies were corrected. Documentation of medical examinations and reexaminations. Inmate and staff interviews. Observation. Documentation of daily monitoring for health and cleanliness.

Food Service Inspection

1-CORE-4A-05 (Mandatory)

(Ref. 4-ALDF-4A-15) **If food services are provided by the facility, there are weekly inspections of all food services areas, including dining and food preparation areas and equipment. Water temperature is checked and recorded daily.**

Comment: None.

Protocols: Written policy and procedure. Inspection forms and formats.
Process Indicators: Observation. Measurement. Inspection reports, completed forms, including documentation that identified deficiencies were corrected.

Food Service Management

1-CORE-4A-06
(Ref. 4-ALDF-4A-17, 4A-18)

Three meals, including at least two hot meals, are prepared, delivered, and served under staff supervision at regular times during each twenty-four hour period, with no more than fourteen hours between the evening meal and breakfast. Variations may be allowed based on weekend and holiday food service demands, provided basic nutritional goals are met.

Comment: None.

Protocols: Written policy and procedure. Meal schedules.
Process Indicators: Observation. Inmate interviews. Records of meals served and times served. Facility records and logs.

PERFORMANCE STANDARD: Hygiene

4B. Inmates maintain acceptable personal hygiene practices.

EXPECTED PRACTICES

Bedding Issue

1-CORE-4B-01
(Ref. 4-ALDF-4B-02)

Inmates are issued suitable, clean bedding and linens. There is provision for linen exchange, including towels, at least weekly.

Comment: None.

Protocols: Written policy and procedure.
Process Indicators: Documentation of issue and exchange.

Clothing

1-CORE-4B-02
(Ref. 4-ALDF-4B-03)

Inmates are issued clothing that is properly fitted and suitable for the climate. There are provisions for inmates to exchange clothing at least twice weekly.

Comment: None.

Protocols: Written policy and procedure.
Process Indicators: Observation. Inmate interviews. Documentation of cleaning and storage. Documentation of clothing issue.

Personal Hygiene

1-CORE-4B-03
(Ref. 4-ALDF-4B-06)

Articles and services necessary for maintaining proper personal hygiene are available to all inmates including items specifically needed for females.

Comment: None.

Protocols: Written policy and procedure.
Process Indicators: Documentation that items are provided. Observation. Inmate interviews.

Plumbing Fixtures

1-CORE-4B-04
(Ref. 4-ALDF-4B-08, 4B-09, 4C-10)

Inmates, including those in medical housing units or infirmaries, have access to showers, toilets, and washbasins with temperature-controlled hot and cold running water twenty-four hours per day. Inmates are able to use toilet facilities without staff assistance when they are confined in their cells/sleeping areas. Water for showers is thermostatically controlled to temperatures ranging from 100 degrees to 120 degrees Fahrenheit.

Comment: None.

Protocols: Written policy and procedure. Facility plans/specifications. Applicable building codes and regulations. Documentation of periodic measurement of water temperature. Inmate grievances. Inmate interviews.
Process Indicators: Observation. Inmate housing records. Measurement. Inspection/ Maintenance records or reports. Observation.

PERFORMANCE STANDARD: Continuum of Health Care Services

4C. **Inmates maintain good health. Inmates have unimpeded access to a continuum of health care services so that their health care needs, including prevention and health education, are met in a timely and efficient manner.**

EXPECTED PRACTICES

Access to Care/Clinical Services

1-CORE-4C-01 (Mandatory)
(Ref. 4-ALDF-4C-01, 4C-02, 4C-03)
At the time of admission/intake, all inmates are informed about procedures to access health services, including any copay requirements, as well as procedures for submitting grievances. Medical care is not denied based on an inmate's ability to pay. There is a process for all inmates to initiate requests for health services on a daily basis. These requests are triaged by qualified health professionals or processed by health-trained persons to ensure that needs are addressed in a timely manner in accordance with the severity of the illness. When the necessary medical, dental, or mental health care is not available at the facility, inmates are referred to and given timely access to the needed clinical services in an other appropriate setting.

Comment: No member of the correctional staff should approve or disapprove inmate requests for health care services. When the facility frequently has non-English speaking inmates, procedures should be explained and written in their language.

Protocols: Written policy and procedures. Inmate handbook. Grievance procedure.
Process Indicators: Documentation that inmates are informed about health care and the grievance system. Inmate grievances. Interviews. Financial records. Sick call request form. A health record. Clinical provider schedules. Observation. Interviews.

Continuity of Care/Referrals

1-CORE-4C-02
(Ref. 4-ALDF-4C-04, 4C-05)
When health care is transferred to providers in the community, appropriate information is shared with the new providers in accordance with consent requirements. Prior to release, inmates with serious health conditions are referred to available community services

Comment: When health care is transferred to providers in the community, appropriate information should be shared with the new providers in accordance with consent requirements. Health care staff should collaborate with security personnel in determining conditions of transportation and necessary security precautions when an inmate needs to be transported to another facility or provider.

Protocols: Written policy and procedure. Referral transfer/consult form.
Process Indicators: Completed referral, transfer, consult forms. Health records. Facility logs. Interviews. Transportation logs. Documentation of annual list review of providers.

Emergency Plan

1-CORE-4C-03 (Mandatory)

(Ref. 4-ALDF-4C-08)

Inmates have access to twenty-four-hour emergency medical, dental, and mental health services, including on-site first aid, basic life support, and transfer to community-based services.

Comment: In the event that primary health services are not available, and particularly in emergency situations, back-up facilities or providers should be predetermined. The plan may include the use of an alternative hospital emergency service or a physician on-call service.

Protocols: Written policy or procedure.
Process Indicators: Designated facility. Provider lists. Transportation logs. Interviews.

Infirmary Care

1-CORE-4C-04

(Ref. 4-ALDF-4C-09)

If infirmary care is provided onsite, it complies with applicable state regulations and local licensing requirements. Provisions include twenty-four-hour emergency on-call consultation with a physician, dentist, and mental health professional.

Comment: An infirmary is a specific area of a health care facility, separate from other housing areas, where inmates are housed and provided health care. Admission and discharge from this area is controlled by medical orders or protocols.

Protocols: Written policy or procedures. Nursing manual. Licensing requirements and regulations.
Process Indicators: Admission and inpatient records. Staffing schedules. Documentation of compliance with licensing requirements and regulations. Observations. Interviews.

Pregnancy Management

1-CORE-4C-05 (Mandatory)

(Ref. 4-ALDF-4C-13)

Pregnant inmates have access to obstetrical services by a qualified provider, including prenatal, peripartum, and postpartum care.

Comment: Management should include family planning services prior to release.

Protocols: Written policy and procedure. Inmate handbook. Contract or agreement.
Process Indicators: Health record entries. Laboratory records. Interviews.

Communicable Disease and Infection Control Program

1-CORE-4C-06 (Mandatory)

(Ref. 4-ALDF-
4C-14, 4C-15,
4C-16, 4C-17,
4C-18)

Communicable diseases, such as tuberculosis, human immunodeficiency virus (HIV) infection, viral hepatitis, Methicillin Resistant Staphylococcal Aureus (MRSA) infection, and influenza are managed in accordance with a written plan approved by the health authority in consultation with local public health officials. The plan includes provisions for the screening, surveillance, treatment, containment, and reporting of infectious diseases. Infection control measures include the availability of personal protective equipment for staff and hand hygiene promotion throughout the facility. Procedures for handling biohazardous waste and decontaminating medical and dental equipment must comply with applicable local, state, and federal regulations.

Comment: Because of their serious nature, methods of transmission, and public sensitivity, these diseases require special attention. Plans for the management of tuberculosis may be based on incidence and prevalence of the disease within the agency's population and the surrounding community.

Protocols: Written policy and procedure, codes, regulations, and treatment guidelines.
Process Indicators: Health records, laboratory, x-ray reports, and logs, chronic care forms, and clinic visit logs. Minutes of communicable disease and infection control committee meetings. Interviews. Documentation of waste pick up, spore count logs, and/or cleaning logs.

Chronic Care

1-CORE-4C-07 (Mandatory)

(Ref. 4-ALDF-
4C-19)

Inmates with chronic medical conditions, such as diabetes, hypertension, and mental illness receive periodic care by a qualified health care provider in accordance with individual treatment plans that include monitoring of medications and laboratory testing.

Comment: Professionally recognized chronic care guidelines are available from disease-specific organizations and various medical and physicians' associations.

Protocols: Written policy and procedure. Chronic care protocols and forms.
Process Indicators: Health records. Chronic care logs. Specialist's schedules.

Dental Care

1-CORE-4C-08
(Ref. 4-ALDF-4C-20)

Routine and emergency dental care is provided to inmates under the direction and supervision of a licensed dentist. Oral health services include access to diagnostic x-rays, treatment of dental pain, development of individual treatment plans, extraction of non-restorable teeth, and referral to a dental specialist, including an oral surgeon.

Comment: As part of the initial health care screening, a dentist or health care personnel, properly trained and designated by the dentist, should perform dental screening. The dental program also should provide inmates with instruction on the proper brushing of the teeth and other dental hygiene measures. The dental examination should include taking or reviewing the inmate's dental history and a full examination of hard and soft tissue of the oral cavity; diagnostic x-rays should be available, if deemed necessary. The examination results should be recorded on a uniform dental record using a numbered system such as the Federation Dental International System.

Protocols: Written policy and procedure. Dental screening by examination forms. Requests to see the dentist.

Process Indicators: Dental records. Admission logs. Referral and consultation records. Dental request forms. Dental interviews with staff.

Health Screens

1-CORE-4C-09 (Mandatory)
(Ref. 4-ALDF-4C-22, 4C-29)

Intake physical and mental health screening commences upon the inmate's arrival at the facility unless there is documentation of a medical screening within the previous 90 days or the inmate is an intrasystem transfer. Screening is conducted by health-trained staff or by qualified health care personnel in accordance with protocols established by the health authority. The screening includes at the least the following:

- **current or past medical conditions, including mental health problems and communicable diseases**
- **current medications, including psychotropics**
- **history of hospitalization, including inpatient psychiatric care**
- **suicidal risk assessment, including suicidal ideation or history of suicidal behavior**
- **use of alcohol and other drugs including potential need for detoxification**
- **dental pain, swelling, or functional impairment**
- **possibility of pregnancy**
- **cognitive or physical impairment**

Observation of the following:

- **behavior, including state of consciousness, mental status, appearance, conduct, tremor, or sweating**
- **body deformities and other physical abnormalities**
- **ease of movement**

- **condition of the skin, including trauma markings, bruises, lesions, jaundice, rashes, infestations, recent tattoos, and needle marks or other indications of injection drug use**
- **symptoms of psychosis, depression, anxiety and/or aggression**

Medical disposition of the inmate:

- **refusal of admission until inmate is medically cleared**
- **cleared for general population**
- **cleared for general population with prompt referral to appropriate medical or mental health care services**
- **referral to appropriate medical or mental health care service for emergency treatment**
- **process for observation for high risk events, such as seizures, detoxification, head wounds, and so forth**

Comment: Health screening is a system of structured inquiry and observation to prevent newly arrived inmates who pose a health or safety threat to themselves or others from being admitted to the general population and to identify inmates who require immediate medical attention. Receiving screening can be performed at the time of admission by health care personnel or by a health-trained correctional officer. Examples of symptoms of serious, infectious or communicable diseases include a chronic cough, lethargy, weakness, weight loss, loss of appetite, fever, or night sweats that are suggestive of such illness.

Protocols: Written policy and procedure. Screening protocols. Mental health screening form.
Process Indicators: Health records. Completed mental health screening forms. Transfer logs. Interviews.

Intra-System Transfer and Health Screening

1-CORE-4C-10 (Mandatory)
(Ref. 4-ALDF-4C-23)   **All intra-system transfer inmates receive a health screening by health-trained or qualified health care personnel, which commences on their arrival at the facility. All findings are recorded on a screening form approved by the health authority. At a minimum, the screening includes the following:**

- **a review of the inmate's medical, dental, and mental health problems**
- **current medications**
- **current treatment plan**

Comment: Health screening of intrasystem transfers is necessary to detect inmates who pose a health or safety threat to themselves or others and who may require immediate health care.

Protocols: Written policy and procedure. Screening form.
Process Indicators: Health records. Completed screening forms. Transfer logs. Interviews.

Health Appraisal

1-CORE-4C-11 (Mandatory)

(Ref. 4-ALDF-4C-24) **A comprehensive physical and mental health appraisal is completed for each inmate within 14 days after arrival at the facility in accordance with protocols established by the health authority, unless a health appraisal has been completed within the previous 90 days. The health appraisal includes the review of the previous receiving screening, a medical history, and physical examination by a qualified health care provider, and an individual treatment plan.**

Comment: Test results, particularly for communicable diseases, should be received and evaluated before an inmate is assigned to housing in the general population. Information regarding the inmate's physical and mental status also may dictate housing and activity assignments. When appropriate, additional investigation should be conducted into alcohol and drug abuse and other related problems.

Protocols: Written policy and procedure. Health appraisal form.
Process Indicators: Health records. Completed health appraisal forms. Transfer logs. Interviews.

Mental Health Program

1-CORE-4C-12 (Mandatory)

(Ref. 4-ALDF-4C-27, 4C-28) **Inmates have access to mental health services as clinically warranted in accordance with protocols established by the health authority that include:**

- **screening for mental health problems**
- **referral to outpatient services, including psychiatric care**
- **crisis intervention and management of acute psychiatric episodes**
- **stabilization of the mentally ill and prevention of psychiatric deterioration in the facility**
- **referral and admission to inpatient facilities**
- **informed consent for treatment**

Comment: An adequate number of qualified staff members should be available to deal directly with inmates who have severe mental health problems and to advise other correctional staff about their contacts with such individuals.

Protocols: Written policy and procedure. Screening form. Job descriptions for mental health personnel.
Process Indicators: Health records. Completed screening forms. Provider qualifications and time and attendance records. Observations. Interviews. Documentation of review by mental health personnel. Interviews.

Suicide Prevention and Intervention

1-CORE-4C-13 (Mandatory)

(Ref. 4-ALDF-4C-32)   **A suicide-prevention program is approved by the health authority and reviewed by the facility or program administrator. The program must include specific procedures for handling intake, screening, identifying, and continually supervising the suicide-prone inmate. All staff responsible for supervising suicide-prone inmates are trained annually on program expectations.**

Comment: None.

Protocols: Written policy and procedures. Training curriculum and lesson plans. Suicide-watch logs or forms.
Process Indicators: Health records. Documentation of staff training. Documentation of suicide watches and critical incident debriefings. Observations. Interviews.

Detoxification

1-CORE-4C-14 (Mandatory)

(Ref. 4-ALDF-4C-36)   **Detoxification from alcohol, opiates, hypnotics, and other stimulants is conducted under medical supervision in accordance with local, state, and federal laws. When performed at the facility, detoxification is prescribed in accordance with clinical protocols approved by the health authority. Specific criteria are established for referring symptomatic inmates suffering from withdrawal or intoxication for more specialized care at a hospital or detoxification center.**

Comment: None.

Protocols: Written policy and procedure. Community contract agreements.
Process Indicators: Health records. Transfer records. Interviews.

Pharmaceuticals

1-CORE-4C-15 (Mandatory)

(Ref. 4-ALDF-4C-38)   **Pharmaceuticals are managed in accordance with policies and procedures approved by the health authority and in compliance with state and federal laws and regulations. The policies require dispensing and administering prescribed medications by qualified personnel, adequate management of controlled medications, and provision of medications to inmates in special management units.**

Comment: The formulary should include all prescription and nonprescription medications stocked in a facility or routinely procured from outside sources. Controlled substances are those classified by the Drug Enforcement Agency as Schedule II-V.

Protocols: Written policy and procedure. Federal and state laws and regulations. Format for documentation of medication, inventory, and storage of medication.
Process Indicators: Health records. Completed medication administration, inventory, and storage forms. Documentation of compliance with federal and state laws.

PERFORMANCE STANDARD: Health Services Staff

4D. Health services are provided in a professionally acceptable manner. Staff are qualified, adequately trained, and demonstrate competency in their assigned duties.

EXPECTED PRACTICES

Health Authority

1-CORE-4D-01 (Mandatory)
(Ref. 4-ALDF-
4D-01)

The facility has a designated health authority with responsibility for health care services pursuant to a written agreement, contract, or job description. The health authority may be a physician, health services administrator, or health agency. When the health authority is other than a physician, final clinical judgments rest with a single, designated, responsible physician. The health authority is authorized and responsible for making decisions about the deployment of health resources and the day-to-day operations of the health services program.

Comment: The health authority and health services administrator may be the same person. The responsibility of the health authority includes arranging for all levels of health services, assuring the quality of all health services, and assuring that inmates have access to them. Health services should ensure the physical and mental well-being of the inmate population and should include medical and dental services, mental health services, nursing care, personal hygiene, dietary services, health education, and attending to environmental conditions. While overall responsibility may be assumed at a central office level, it is essential that each facility have an onsite health services administrator.

Protocols: Written policy and procedure. Sample agreement or contract requirements with health care provider or authority. Job description.
Process Indicators: Documentation of health authority designation. Contract. Billing records. Interviews. Documentation of mission statement, operational policies and procedures, scope of services and required personnel, coordination of care, and a quality management program.

Health Care Quarterly Meetings

1-CORE-4D-02
(Ref. 4-ALDF-
7D-25)

The health authority meets with the facility administrator at least quarterly.

Comment: Minutes of the quarterly administrative meetings may be used to meet the requirements for a quarterly report.

Protocols: Written policy and procedure.
Process Indicators: Documentation of meetings. Minutes and reports. Interviews.

Provision of Treatment

1-CORE-4D-03 (Mandatory)

(Ref. 4-ALDF-
4D-02)

Clinical decisions are the sole province of the responsible clinician and are not countermanded by non-clinicians.

Comment: The provision of health care is a joint effort of administrators and health care providers and can be achieved only through mutual trust and cooperation. The health authority arranges for the availability of health care services; the responsible clinician determines what services are needed; the official responsible for the facility provides the administrative support for making the services accessible to inmates.

Protocols: Written policy and procedure.
Process Indicators: Health record entries. Inmate grievances. Interviews.

Personnel Qualifications/Credentials

1-CORE-4D-04 (Mandatory)

(Ref. 4-ALDF-
4D-03, 4D-05)

All health care professional staff comply with applicable state and federal licensure, certification, or registration requirements. Verification of current credentials is on file at the facility. Health care staff work in accordance with profession-specific job descriptions approved by the health authority. If inmates are assessed or treated by nonlicensed health care personnel, the care is provided pursuant to written standing or direct orders by personnel authorized to give such orders.

Comment: Standing medical orders are for the definitive treatment of identified conditions and for the on-site emergency treatment of any person having such condition. Direct orders are those written specifically for the treatment of one person's particular condition.

Protocols: Written policy and procedures. Job descriptions. Standing orders. Copies of licensure requirements.
Process Indicators: Personnel records. Copies of credentials or licensure. Documentation of compliance with standing orders. Health record entries. Interviews. Documentation of current credentials.

Emergency Response

1-CORE-4D-05 (Mandatory)
(Ref. 4-ALDF-
4D-08)

Emergency medical care, including first aid and basic life support, is provided by all health care professionals and those health-trained correctional staff specifically designated by the facility administrator. All staff responding to medical emergencies are certified in cardiopulmonary resuscitation (CPR) in accordance with the recommendations of the certifying health organization. The health authority approves policies and procedures that ensure that emergency supplies and equipment, including automatic external defibrillators (AEDs), are readily available and in working order.

Comment: The facility administrator and the health care authority may designate those correctional officers who have responsibility for responding to health care emergencies. Staff not physically able to perform CPR are exempt from the expected practice.

Protocols: Written policy and procedure. Lesson plans and curriculum.
Process Indicators: Verification of training. Records and certificates. Interviews.

Notification

1-CORE-4D-06
(Ref. 4-ALDF-
4D-12)

Individuals designated by an inmate are notified in case of serious illness, serious injury, or death, unless security reasons dictate otherwise.

Comment: The persons to be notified should be designated in writing as part of the facility's admissions procedures.

Protocols: Written policy and procedure.
Process Indicators: Notification records.

Confidentiality

1-CORE-4D-07 (Mandatory)
(Ref. 4-ALDF-
4D-13, 4D-14)

Information about an inmate's health status is confidential. Nonmedical staff only have access to specific medical information on a "need to know" basis in order to preserve the health and safety of the specific inmate, other inmates, volunteers, visitors, or correctional staff. The active health record is maintained separately from the confinement case record and access is controlled in accordance with state and federal laws.

Comment: The principle of confidentiality protects inmate patients from disclosure of confidences entrusted to a health care provider during the course of treatment.

Protocols: Policy and procedure.
Process Indicators: Observation. Interviews.

Informed Consent

1-CORE-4D-08 (Mandatory)
(Ref. 4-ALDF-4D-15)   **Informed consent standards of the jurisdiction are observed and documented for inmate care in a language understood by the inmate. In the case of minors, the informed consent of a parent, guardian, or a legal custodian applies, when required by law. Inmates routinely have the right to refuse medical interventions. When health care is rendered against the inmate's will, it is in accordance with state and federal laws and regulations.**

Comment: None.

Protocols: Written policy and procedure. Consent or authorization forms.
Process Indicators: Health records. Completed consent forms. Completed refusal forms. Interviews.

Involuntary Administration

1-CORE-4D-09 (Mandatory)
(Ref. 4-ALDF-4D-17)   **Involuntary administration of psychotropic medication(s) to inmates is authorized by a physician and provided in accordance with policies and procedures approved by the health authority, and in accordance with applicable laws and regulations of the jurisdiction.**

Comment: None.

Protocols: Written policy and procedure. Laws and regulations.
Process Indicators: A health record. Interviews.

Research

1-CORE-4D-10 (Mandatory)
(Ref. 4-ALDF-4D-18)   **The use of inmates in medical, pharmaceutical, or cosmetic experiments is prohibited. This expected practice does not preclude inmate access to investigational medications on a case-by-case basis for therapeutic purposes in accordance with state and federal regulations.**

Comment: Experimental programs include aversive conditioning, psychosurgery, and the application of cosmetic substances being tested prior to sale to the general public.

Protocols: Written policy and procedure. Laws and regulations.
Process Indicators: Health records. Interviews.

Privacy

1-CORE-4D-11
(Ref. 4-ALDF-4D-19)

Health care encounters, including medical and mental health interviews, examinations, and procedures are conducted in a setting that respects the inmates' privacy.

Comment: None.

Protocols: Written policy and procedure. Facility diagram.
Process Indicators: Observation. Interviews.

Use of Restraints

1-CORE-4D-12 (Mandatory)
(Ref. 4-ALDF-4D-21)

Restraints on inmates for medical and psychiatric purposes are only applied in accordance with policies and procedures approved by the health authority, including:

- **conditions under which restraints may be applied**
- **types of restraints to be applied**
- **identification of a qualified medical or mental health professional who may authorize the use of restraints after reaching the conclusion that less intrusive measures are not a viable alternative**
- **monitoring procedures**
- **length of time restraints are to be applied**
- **documentation of efforts for less restrictive treatment alternatives**
- **an after-incident review.**

Comment: None.

Protocols: Written policy and procedure. Monitoring form.
Process Indicators: Health records. Restraint logs. Completed monitoring forms. List of providers authorized to order restraints. Interviews.

Sexual Assault

1-CORE-4D-13
(Ref. 4-ALDF-2A-29)

Information is provided to inmates about sexual abuse/assault including:

- **prevention/intervention**
- **self-protection**
- **reporting sexual abuse/assault**
- **treatment and counseling**

The information is communicated orally and in writing, in a language clearly understood by the inmate, upon arrival at the facility.

Comment: None.

Protocols: Policy and procedure
Process Indicators: Observation, inmate interviews, inmate handbook, completed receipt forms.

Sexual Conduct of Staff

1-CORE-4D-14
(Ref. 4-ALDF-4D-22-1, 4D-22-5)

Sexual conduct between staff and detainees, volunteers or contract personnel and detainees, regardless of consensual status, is prohibited and subject to administrative, disciplinary, and criminal sanctions.

Comment: None.

Protocols: Written policy and procedure.
Process Indicators: Screening records. Admission logs. Classification records. Documentation of staff awareness, for example, annual in-service training curriculum.

Investigation of Sexual Assault

1-CORE-4D-15
(Ref. 4-ALDF-4D-22-2)

An investigation is conducted and documented whenever a sexual assault or threat is reported.

Comment: The agency should report occurrences/allegations of sexual assault or threat in accordance with the laws of the jurisdiction. The investigation may be limited by what is allowed by the laws of the jurisdiction.

Protocols: Written policy and procedure.
Process Indicators: Referral records. Investigative reports.

Victims of Sexual Assault

1-CORE-4D-16 (Mandatory)
(Ref. 4-ALDF-
4D-22-6)

Victims of sexual assault are referred under appropriate security provisions to a community facility for treatment and gathering of evidence. If these procedures are performed in-house, the following guidelines are used:

- **A history is taken by health care professionals who conduct an examination to document the extent of physical injury and to determine if referral to another medical facility is indicated. With the victim's consent, the examination includes collection of evidence from the victim, using a kit approved by the appropriate authority.**
- **Provision is made for testing for sexually transmitted diseases (for example HIV, gonorrhea, hepatitis, and other diseases) and counseling, as appropriate.**
- **Prophylactic treatment and follow-up for sexually transmitted diseases are offered to all victims, as appropriate.**
- **Following the physical examination, there is availability of an evaluation by a mental health professional to assess the need for crisis intervention counseling and long-term follow-up.**
- **A report is made to the facility administrator or designee to assure separation of the victim from his or her assailant.**

Comment: None.

Protocols: Written policy and procedure. Referral documents.
Process Indicators: Completed referral forms. Medical records. Classification records.

Inmate Death/Health Care Internal Review and Quality Assurance

1-CORE-4D-17 (Mandatory)
(Ref. 4-ALDF-
4D-23, 4D-24)

The health authority approves policies and procedures for identifying and evaluating major risk-management events related to inmate health care, including inmate deaths, preventable adverse outcomes, and serious medication errors.

Comment: The medical examiner or coroner should be notified of an inmate's death immediately. A postmortem examination should be performed, according to the laws of the jurisdiction, if the cause of death is unknown, the death occurred under suspicious circumstances, or the inmate was not under current medical care. Reports can be facilitated by regular participation of the facility administrator, health administrator, and responsible physician. It is suggested that a physician act as the supervisor of the program. Evaluating data should result in more effective access, improved quality of care, and better utilization of resources.

Protocols: Written policy and procedure. Record review format.
Process Indicators: Documentation of completed record review. Quality improvement committee minutes. Quarterly report. Interviews.

Health Records

1-CORE-4D-18
(Ref. 4-ALDF-
4D-26)

An individual health record is maintained for all inmates in accordance with policies and procedures established by the health authority and in accordance with applicable state and federal regulations. The method of recording entries in the records, the form and format of the records, and the procedures for their maintenance and safekeeping are approved by the health authority. The health record is made available to, and is used for documentation by all practitioners.

Comment: The receiving screening form should become a part of the record at the time of the first health encounter. Records may be maintained electronically. Examples of health service reports include emergency department, dental, mental health, telemedicine, or other consultations.

Protocols: Policy and procedure. Health record forms.
Process Indicators: Health records. Completed forms. Interviews.

5. Program and Activity

GOAL: Help inmates to successfully return to the community and reduce the negative effects of confinement.

PERFORMANCE STANDARD: Inmate Opportunities for Improvement

5A. Inmates have opportunities to improve themselves while confined.

EXPECTED PRACTICES

Programs and Services

1-CORE-5A-01
(Ref. 4-ALDF-
5A-01)

Inmate programs, services and counseling are available. Community resources are used to supplement these programs and services.

Comment: None.

Protocols: Written policy and procedure. Facility program and activity schedule.
Process Indicators: Activity schedules. Facility logs. Inmate interviews. Observation.

PERFORMANCE STANDARD: Family and Community Ties

5B. Inmates maintain ties with their families and the community.

EXPECTED PRACTICES

Visiting

1-CORE-5B-01
(Ref. 4-ALDF-
5B-01, 5B-02,
5B-03, 5B-04)

The number of visitors an inmate may receive and the length of visits are limited only by the facility's schedule, space, and personnel constraints or when there are substantial reasons to justify such limitations. Visitors are required to identify themselves and register on entry into the facility. Conditions under which visits may be denied and visitors may be searched are defined in writing. Provisions are made for special visits.

Comment: None.

Protocols: Written policy and procedure. Facility program, service plan and activity schedule. Staffing plan. Contracts for service.
Process Indicators: Activity schedules. Facility logs. Inmate interviews. Observation. Documentation of the identification and use of community resources. Review of contractual services. Program records. Inmate interviews.

Mail

1-CORE-5B-02
(Ref. 4-ALDF-
5B-06, 5B-08,
5B-09)

Inmates may send and receive mail. Indigent inmates receive a specified postage allowance. Both incoming and outgoing mail may be opened to intercept cash, checks, and money orders and inspected for contraband. Mail is read, censored, or rejected based on legitimate facility interests of order and security. Inmates are notified in writing when incoming or outgoing letters are withheld in part or in full. Staff, in the presence of the inmate, may be allowed to inspect outgoing privileged mail for contraband before it is sealed. Mail to inmates from this privileged class of persons and organizations may be opened only to inspect for contraband and only in the presence of the inmate, unless waived in writing, or in circumstances, which may indicate contamination.

Comment: Suspicious mail may include packages and letters unusual in appearance or which appear different from mail normally received or sent by the individual; packages and letters of a size or shape not customarily received or sent by the individual; packages and letters with a city and/or state postmark that is different from the return address; or packages and letters that leak, are stained, or emit a strange or unusual odor, or which have a powdery residue.

Protocols: Written policy and procedure. Budget forms. Inmate handbook.
Process Indicators: Documentation of postage provided to indigent inmates. Mail logs and records. Documentation of justification for reading, censoring, or rejecting mail. Documentation that inmates are notified when mail is withheld. Staff and inmate interviews. Observation.

Telephone

1-CORE-5B-03
(Ref. 4-ALDF-
5B-11)

Inmates are provided with access to telephones.

Comment: None.

Protocols: Written policy and procedure. Facility plans/specifications.
Process Indicators: Observation. Inmate interviews. Documentation of inmate access to telephones.

Release

1-CORE-5B-04
(Ref. 4-ALDF-
5B-18)

Procedures for releasing inmates from the facility include, but are not limited to, the following:

- **identification of outstanding warrants, wants, or detainers**
- **verification of identity**
- **verification of release papers**
- **completion of release arrangements, including notification of the parole authorities in the jurisdiction of release, if required**
- **return of personal property**
- **provision of a listing of available community resources**
- **provision of medication as directed by the health authority**

Comment: None.

Protocols: Written policy and procedure. Release forms and procedures.
Process Indicators: Completed release forms and documents. Facility records and logs. Inmate records. Observation.

PERFORMANCE STANDARD: Programs

5C. The negative impact of confinement is reduced.

EXPECTED PRACTICES

Exercise and Recreation Access

1-CORE-5C-01
(Ref. 4-ALDF-5C-01, 5C-02)   **Inmates have access to exercise and recreation opportunities. When available, at least one hour daily is outside the cell or outdoors when weather permits.** *Comment*: None.

Protocols: Written policy and procedure. Facility plans/specifications. Schedules.
Process Indicators: Observation. Measurement. Facility logs and activity records.

Outdoor and Covered/Enclosed Recreation Area

1-CORE-5C-02
(Ref. 4-ALDF-5C-03)   **Both outdoor and covered/enclosed exercise areas for general population inmates are provided in sufficient number to ensure that each inmate is offered at least one hour of access daily. Use of outdoor areas is preferred, but covered/enclosed are available for use in inclement weather. Covered/enclosed areas may be designed for multiple uses as long as the design and furnishings do not interfere with scheduled exercise activities. The minimum space requirements for exercise areas are as follows:**

- **Outdoor exercise areas in facilities where 100 or more inmates utilize one recreation area—15 square feet per inmate for the maximum number of inmates expected to use the space at one time, but not less than 1,500 square feet of unencumbered space**
- **Outdoor exercise areas in facilities where less than 100 inmates have unlimited access to an individual recreation area—15 square feet per inmate for the maximum number of inmates expected to use the space at one time, but not less than 750 square feet of unencumbered space**
- **Covered/enclosed exercise areas in facilities where 100 or more inmates utilize one recreation area have 15 square feet per inmate for the maximum number of inmates expected to use the space at one time, but not less than 1,000 square feet of unencumbered space**
- **Covered/enclosed exercise areas in facilities where less than 100 inmates utilize one recreation area have 15 square feet per inmate for the maximum number of inmates expected to use the space at one time, but not less than 500 square feet of unencumbered space.**

Comment: Exercise/recreation spaces are not the same as dayrooms, although dayrooms can provide added opportunities for some exercise and recreation activities. The standard establishes performance requirements for exercise spaces, offering design and operational flexibility. It allows facilities in some climates to cover and/or enclose a yard, while others will have to provide indoor space. These spaces do not have to be "indoors" but must be fully functional when the outdoor areas are not feasible for use.

Protocols: Written policy and procedure. Facility plans/specifications. Schedules.
Process Indicators: Observation. Measurement. Facility logs and activity records.

Segregated Inmates

1-CORE-5C-03
(Ref. 4-ALDF-5C-04)

Segregated inmates have access to both outdoor and covered/enclosed exercise areas. The minimum space requirements for outdoor and covered/enclosed exercise areas for segregation units are as follows:

- **Group yard modules--15 square feet per inmate expected to use the space at one time, but not less than 500 square feet of unencumbered space**
- **Individual yard modules–180 square feet of unencumbered space**

In cases where cover is not provided to mitigate the inclement weather, appropriate weather-related equipment and attire should be made available to the inmates who desire to take advantage of their authorized exercise time.

Comment: None.

Protocols: Written policy and procedure. Facility plans/specifications. Schedules.
Process Indicators: Observation. Measurement. Facility logs and activity records.

Library Services

1-CORE-5C-04
(Ref. 4-ALDF-5C-05)

Library services are available to inmates.

Comment: None.

Protocols: Written policy and procedure. Activity schedule.
Process Indicators: Observation. Inmate interviews. Qualifications of staff member.

Work and Correctional Industries

1-CORE-5C-05 (Mandatory)
(Ref. 4-ALDF-5C-11)

Inmate working conditions comply with all applicable federal, state, or local work safety laws and regulations.

Comment: None.

Protocols: Written policy and procedure. Applicable laws and regulations.
Process Indicators: External inspection reports, completed forms, including documentation that identified deficiencies were corrected. Work records. Inmate and staff interviews.

Religious Programs

1-CORE-5C-06
(Ref. 4-ALDF-5C-17)

Inmates have the opportunity to participate in practices of their religious faith consistent with existing state and federal statutes.

Comment: None.

Protocols: Written policy and procedure.
Process Indicators: Documentation of inmate religious activities. Documentation of reasons for limitations. Chaplain interviews. Inmate interviews.

Commissary/Canteen

1-CORE-5C-07
(Ref. 4-ALDF-5C-25)

An inmate commissary or canteen may be available from which inmates can purchase approved items that are not furnished by the facility. The commissary/canteen's operations are strictly controlled using standard accounting procedures.

Comment: None.

Protocols: Written policy and procedure. Commissary forms and formats. Fiscal procedures. Budgets.
Process Indicators: Commissary records. Budgets.

6. Justice

GOAL: *Treat inmates fairly and respect their legal rights. Provide services that hold inmates accountable for their actions, and encourage them to make restitution to their victims and the community.*

PERFORMANCE STANDARD: Inmates' Rights

6A. Inmates' rights are not violated.

EXPECTED PRACTICES

Access to Courts

1-CORE-6A-01
(Ref. 4-ALDF-
6A-01)

The right of inmates to have access to courts is ensured.

Comment: None.

Protocols: Written policy and procedure.
Process Indicators: Facility logs. Inmate interviews. Attorney interviews.

Access to Counsel

1-CORE-6A-02
(Ref. 4-ALDF-
6A-02)

Inmate access to counsel is ensured. Such contact includes, but is not limited to telephone communications, uncensored correspondence, and visits.

Comment: None.

Protocols: Written policy and procedure.
Process Indicators: Inmate interviews. Facility log. Attorney interviews. Observation.

Access to Legal Materials

1-CORE-6A-03
(Ref. 4-ALDF-
6A-03)

Inmates have access to legal materials.

Comment: None.

Protocols: Written policy and procedure. Legal assistance/resources plan.
Process Indicators: Observation. Facility logs. Inmate interviews.

Communications/Telephone

1-CORE-6A-04
(Ref. 4-ALDF-6A-05)

New inmates are allowed the opportunity to complete at least one telephone call during the admission process and are assisted, as needed, to notify persons of their admission to custody.

Comment: None.

Protocols: Written policy and procedure.
Process Indicators: Observation. Intake records. Inmate interviews.

Foreign Nationals

1-CORE-6A-05
(Ref. 4-ALDF-6A-06)

Foreign nationals have access to the diplomatic representative of their country of citizenship.

Comment: None.

Protocols: Written policy and procedure.
Process Indicators: Inmate interviews. Staff interviews.

Protection from Abuse

1-CORE-6A-06 (Mandatory)
(Ref. 4-ALDF-6A-07)

Inmates are not subjected to personal abuse, corporal punishment, personal injury, disease, property damage, or harassment.

Comment: None.

Protocols: Written policy and procedure. Training curricula.
Process Indicators: Facility logs. Incident reports. Inmate interviews. Staff training records.

Grooming

1-CORE-6A-07
(Ref. 4-ALDF-
6A-08)

Inmates are allowed freedom in personal grooming except when a valid governmental interest justifies otherwise.

Comment: None.

Protocols: Written policy and procedure. Grooming regulations. Inmate handbook.
Process Indicators: Documentation of instances in which personal grooming choices were denied. Observation. Inmate interviews.

Indigence

1-CORE-6A-08
(Ref. 4-ALDF-
6A-09)

An indigent inmate's access to health care, programs, services, and activities is not precluded by inability to pay.

Comment: None.

Protocols: Written policy and procedure. Definition of indigence.
Process Indicators: Inmate interviews. Records and logs. Inmate accounts.

PERFORMANCE STANDARD: Fair Treatment of Inmates

6B. Inmates are treated fairly.

EXPECTED PRACTICES

Grievance Procedure

1-CORE-6B-01
(Ref. 4-ALDF-6B-01)

An inmate grievance procedure is made available to all inmates and includes at least one level of appeal.

Comment: None.

Protocols: Written policy and procedure. Grievance procedure. Inmate handbook.
Process Indicators: Grievance records. Inmate interviews.

Discrimination

1-CORE-6B-02
(Ref. 4-ALDF-6B-02, 6B-03)

There is no discrimination regarding administrative decisions or program access based on an inmate's race, religion, national origin, gender, sexual orientation, or disability. When both males and females are housed in the same facility, available services and programs are comparable.

Comment: None.

Protocols: Written policy and procedure. Program and service descriptions and eligibility requirements. Inmate handbook.
Process Indicators: Inmate interviews. Facility records. Grievances. Activity logs. Program records. Staff and inmate interviews.

Disabled Inmates

1-CORE-6B-03
(Ref. 4-ALDF-6B-04)

Inmates with disabilities, including temporary disabilities, are housed and managed in a manner that provides for their safety and security. Housing used by inmates with disabilities, including temporary disabilities, is designed for their use and provides for integration with other inmates. Program and service areas are accessible to inmates with disabilities.

Comment: Temporary disabilities are conditions that can be treated with an expectation of healing. Temporary disabilities are not the result of chronic conditions, are short-term in nature, and resolve over time.

Protocols: Written policy/procedure. Facility plans/specifications.
Process Indicators: Inmate records. Observation. Interviews. Inmate health records.

PERFORMANCE STANDARD: Due Process for Inmates

6C. **Alleged rule violations are handled in a manner that provides inmates with appropriate procedural safeguards.**

EXPECTED PRACTICES

Inmate Discipline

Written Guidelines

1-CORE-6C-01
(Ref. 4-ALDF-
6C-01)

There are written guidelines for resolving minor inmate infractions. Serious infractions are handled consistent with the requirements for limited due process.

Comment: None.

Protocols: Written policy and procedure. Disciplinary guidelines.
Process Indicators: None.

Disciplinary Report

1-CORE-6C-02
(Ref. 4-ALDF-
6C-03)

When rule violations require formal resolutions, a staff member prepares a disciplinary report that describes the alleged violation and forwards it to the designated supervisor.

Comment: None.

Protocols: Written policy and procedure. Disciplinary forms.
Process Indicators: Completed disciplinary forms. Inmate records.

Written Statement

1-CORE-6C-03
(Ref. 4-ALDF-
6C-07, 6C-11)

An inmate charged with a rule violation receives a written statement of the charge(s), including a description of the incident and specific rules violated. The inmate is given the statement at the same time the disciplinary report is filed with the disciplinary committee but no less than 24 hours prior to the disciplinary hearing. The hearing, conducted by an impartial person or panel of persons, may only be held in less than 24 hours, with the inmate's written consent. A record of the proceedings is made and retained.

Comment: None.

Protocols: Written policy and procedure. Disciplinary forms.
Process Indicators: Disciplinary records. Inmate records.

Hearing

1-CORE-6C-04
(Ref. 4-ALDF-
6C-08, 6C-18)   **An inmate charged with rule violations is present at the hearing, unless the inmate waives that right in writing or through behavior. An inmate may be excluded during testimony. An inmate's absence or exclusion is documented. Inmates have an opportunity to appeal disciplinary decisions.**

Comment: None.

Protocols: Written policy and procedure. Waiver form.
Process Indicators: Disciplinary records. Inmate records. Documentation of absence. Inmate interviews. Staff interviews.

7. Administration and Management

GOAL: Administer and manage the facility in a professional and responsible manner, consistent with legal requirements.

PERFORMANCE STANDARD: Recruitment, Retention, and Promotion

7B. Staff, contractors, and volunteers demonstrate competency in their assigned duties.

EXPECTED PRACTICES

Selection, Retention, and Promotion

1-CORE-7B-01
(Ref. 4-ALDF-7B-03)

A criminal record check is conducted on all new employees, contractors, and volunteers prior to their assuming duties to identify if there are criminal convictions that have a specific relationship to job performance. This record check includes comprehensive identifier information to be collected and run against law enforcement indices. If suspect information on matters with potential terrorism connections is returned on a desirable applicant, it is forwarded to the local Joint Terrorism Task Force (JTTF) or another similar agency.

Comment: None.

Protocols: Written policy and procedure.
Process Indicators: Personnel records.

Training and Staff Development

Orientation

1-CORE-7B-02
(Ref. 4-ALDF-7B-05)

Prior to assuming duties, each employee is provided with an orientation, which may include:

- **working conditions**
- **code of ethics**
- **personnel policy manual**
- **employees' rights and responsibilities**
- **overview of the criminal justice system**
- **tour of the facility**
- **facility goals and objectives**
- **facility organization**
- **staff rules and regulations**
- **personnel policies**
- **program overview**

Comment: Orientation is distinct from training because it acquaints personnel with the setting in which they will be working but does not necessarily address the knowledge, skills, and abilities needed to implement assigned duties.

Protocols: Written policy and procedure. Orientation materials and schedule.
Process Indicators: Personnel records. Staff interviews.

Annual Training

1-CORE-7B-03
(Ref. 4-ALDF-7B-08)

All professional, support, clerical, and health care employees, including contractors, receive continuing annual training, which may include:

- **security procedures and regulations**
- **supervision of inmates**
- **signs of suicide risk**
- **suicide precautions**
- **use-of-force regulations and tactics**
- **report writing**
- **inmate rules and regulations**
- **key control**
- **rights and responsibilities of inmates**
- **safety procedures**
- **all emergency plans and procedures**
- **interpersonal relations**
- **social/cultural lifestyles of the inmate population**
- **cultural diversity**
- **CPR/first aid**

- **counseling techniques**
- **sexual harassment/sexual misconduct awareness**
- **purpose, goals, policies, and procedures for the facility and parent agency**
- **security and contraband regulations**
- **appropriate conduct with inmates**
- **responsibilities and rights of employees**
- **universal precautions**
- **occupational exposure**
- **personal protective equipment**
- **bio-hazardous waste disposal**
- **overview of the correctional field**

Comment: None.

Protocols: Written policy and procedure. Job descriptions. Training curriculum. Training record forms and formats.
Process Indicators: Personnel records. Training records.

Training Prior to Assuming Duties

1-CORE-7B-04
(Ref. 4-ALDF-7B-10)

Prior to assuming duties, all correctional officers receive training in the facility under the supervision of a qualified officer. Training may include:

- **facility policies and procedures**
- **suicide prevention**
- **use of force**
- **report writing**
- **inmate rules and regulations**
- **key control**
- **emergency plans and procedures**
- **cultural diversity**
- **communication skills**
- **cardiopulmonary resuscitation (CPR) /first aid**
- **sexual misconduct**

Comment: These training requirements apply to all correctional officers, whether they are full-time or part-time.

Protocols: Written policy and procedure. Job descriptions. Training curriculum. Training record forms and formats.
Process Indicators: Personnel records. Training records.

In-Service Training

1-CORE-7B-05
(Ref. 4-ALDF-7B-10-1)

In each subsequent year of employment, correctional officers receive documented in-service training in critical areas of the operation.

Comment: This training will enable employees to sharpen skills, maintain certification and keep abreast of changes in policies, procedures, and legislation, judicial, or executive sessions.

Protocols: Written policy and procedure. Job descriptions. Training curriculum. Training record forms and formats.
Process Indicators: Personnel records. Training records.

Weapons Training

1-CORE-7B-06 (Mandatory)
(Ref. 4-ALDF-7B-15)

All personnel authorized to use firearms and less-than-lethal weapons must demonstrate competency in their use at least annually. Training includes decontamination procedures for individuals exposed to chemical agents.

Comment: None.

Protocols: Written policy and procedure. Job descriptions. Training curriculum. Training record forms and formats.
Process Indicators: Personnel records. Training records.

PERFORMANCE STANDARD: Facility Administration

7D. The facility is administered efficiently and responsibly.

EXPECTED PRACTICES

Organization

**1-CORE-7D-01
(Ref. 4-ALDF-
7D-06, 7D-08)**

Written policies and procedures describe all facets of facility operation, maintenance, and administration, are reviewed annually and updated, as needed. New or revised policies and procedures are disseminated to staff, and, where appropriate, to contractors, volunteers, and inmates, prior to implementation.

Comment: None.

Protocols: Written policy and procedure. Policy and procedure manual. Distribution lists. Dissemination plan.
Process Indicators: Documentation of annual review. Documentation of timely dissemination.

Financial Practices

**1-CORE-7D-02
(Ref. 4-ALDF-
7D-10)**

The facility administrator prepares and submits an annual budget that requests necessary resources for facility operations and programs.

Comment: None.

Protocols: Written policy and procedure. Budget.
Process Indicators: Staff interviews.

Inmate Funds

**1-CORE-7D-03
(Ref. 4-ALDF-
7D-16)**

Procedures govern the operation of any fund established for inmates. Any interest earned on monies, other than operating funds, accrues to the benefit of the inmates.

Comment: None.

Protocols: Written policy and procedure. Budgets.
Process Indicators: Inmate records. Financial records. Budgets.

Inmate Records

1-CORE-7D-04
(Ref. 4-ALDF-7D-20)

The facility maintains custody records on all inmates committed or assigned to the facility, which include but are not limited to the following:

- **intake/booking information**
- **court-generated background information**
- **cash and property receipts**
- **reports of disciplinary actions, grievances, incidents, or crime(s) committed while in custody**
- **disposition of court hearings**
- **records of program participation**
- **work assignments**
- **classification records**

Inmates have reasonable access to information in their records. Access is only limited due to safety or security concerns for the inmate, other inmates, or the facility. The contents of inmate records are identified and separated according to a format approved by the facility administrator.

Comment: None.

Protocols: Written policy and procedure. Forms. File organization format.
Process Indicators: Inmate records and files.

PERFORMANCE STANDARD: Staff Treatment

7E.   Staff are treated fairly.

EXPECTED PRACTICES

Facility and Equipment/Reasonable Accommodation

1-CORE-7E-01
(Ref. 4-ALDF-7E-05)

Reasonable accommodation is made to ensure that all parts of the facility that are accessible to the public are accessible and usable by staff and visitors with disabilities.

Comment: None.

Protocols: Written policy and procedure. Facility plans/specifications.
Process Indicators: Observation.

Appendix A

Guidelines for Institution Security Levels

The following descriptions illustrate the numbers and types of barriers that separate inmates from the community. These guidelines are designed for illustrative purposes. Segments may be interchanged to compensate for strengths or weaknesses in other segments. Some agencies and systems use more or less than three levels of security. For those systems, these guidelines can be adjusted.

SECURITY ELEMENTS	SECURITY LEVELS		
	I (Minimum)	II (Medium)	III (Maximum)
Housing	Dormitories, cubicles, or rooms	Rooms and/or multiple occupancy cells and/or dormitories	Single cells, very secure, with heavy-duty hardware
Perimeter Security	None, or single fence; occasional patrol	Double fence; electric alarm system; patrol of perimeter or towers	A combination of double fence, wall, towers, and/or constant armed perimeter surveillance; and/or an electronic alarm system
Internal Security Measures	Inmate census taken at least three times daily	Inmate movement is controlled by pass system. Formal census is taken at least four times daily, plus frequent informal censuses.	Formal census is taken at least five times daily. Capability to quickly separate the inmates into smaller groups. Inmates are directly supervised and/or escorted when outside the cellhouse or living area.

Appendix B

Classification Guidelines

The following descriptions illustrate behavior characteristics typical of inmate-custody levels.

Typical Behavior Patterns* for Various Levels of Custody for Inmates in a Correctional Facility

TYPICAL BEHAVIOR PATTERNS	CUSTODY LEVELS		
	I (Minimum)	II (Medium)	III (Maximum)
Risk of Escape	No history of escape or escape attempts from secure or nonsecure settings (within past five years). Length of sentence is three years or less to projected release date.	No escape history (including flight from custody) during past seven years. No history of escape attempts from a secure setting (within past five years). Length of sentence is five years or less to projected release date.	Conduct that indicates high probability of escape attempts. History of escape or escape attempts from secure setting during the past 10 years. Length of sentence is 10 years or more to projected release date.
Behavior	No history of violent behavior (within past five years). No pattern of threats or violence.	No history of institution violence involving weapons or serious injury (within past five years). No history of assault on staff (within past five years). No pattern of serious institutional misconduct. No active participation in prison gangs.	Recent history of violent crimes and/or violent institutional conduct within past five years. Active membership in gangs/groups advocating violence. Serious assault on staff.

*These characteristics are used only as guidelines; decisions should also be based on evaluations by the classification committee (including mental health and security staff) to determine the proper custody-level assignment. Inmates also may be assigned increased or decreased levels of custody based on behavior during incarceration or extenuating circumstances relating to the behavior pattern.

Definition of Direct Supervision

- A method of inmate management that ensures continuing direct contact between inmates and staff by posting an officer(s) inside each housing unit.
- Officers in general housing units are not separated from inmates by a physical barrier.
- Officers provide frequent, nonscheduled observation of and personal interaction with inmates.

Appendix C

Definition of "Qualified Individual" for Safety and Sanitation Inspections

Several standards refer to documentation and inspections by "qualified individuals." (For example, Building and Safety Codes, Fire Safety, Food Service, Sanitation and Hygiene, and Work and Correctional Industries standards.) Such persons also may be referred to as an "independent, qualified source," "qualified departmental staff member," "qualified designee," or "qualified fire and safety officer."

A "qualified individual" is a person whose training, education, and/or experience specifically qualifies him or her to do the job indicated in the standard.

I. GENERAL REQUIREMENTS

When a standard calls for inspections, the individual conducting them needs to be trained in the application of appropriate codes and regulations. Standards do not specify the number of hours of training required, as this is determined in part by the tasks assigned. At a minimum, though, the qualified individual must (1) be familiar with the applicable codes and regulations and their requirements; (2) be able to use the appropriate instruments for measuring and documenting code compliance; (3) be able to complete checklists and prepare the necessary reports; and (4) have the authority to make corrections when deficiencies are found.

Training is often obtained from code officials or inspectors (fire marshals, building officials); government agencies that have statutory authority for inspections in a particular area (health department, labor department); or private organizations, such as the National Fire Protection Association. Often the individual obtains written certification or approval from these authorities to conduct in-house inspections. When trained and certified by the above sources to do so, a central office specialist may train and assist facility staff to conduct inspections.

II. SPECIFIC REQUIREMENTS

A. Authority Having Jurisdiction

The term "authority having jurisdiction" is defined as follows:

The authority having jurisdiction must be knowledgeable about the requirements of the National Fire Protection Life Safety Code. The authority having jurisdiction may be a federal, state, local, or other regional department or individual, such as the fire chief, fire marshal, chief of a fire prevention bureau, labor department, health department, building official, electrical inspector, or others with statutory authority. The authority having jurisdiction may be employed by the department/agency, provided that he or she is not under the authority of the facility administrator and that the report generated is referred to higher authorities within the department/ agency independent of influence by the facility administrator or staff. This rule applies no matter who generates the report. The definition also applies to the terms "independent, qualified source" and "independent, outside source."

B. Inspections

Qualified individuals conducting the monthly and weekly inspections required in the standards may be institutional staff members.

The qualified individual responsible for conducting monthly inspections (for example, fire and safety officer, safety/sanitation specialist) may be an institutional staff member trained in the application of jurisdictional codes and regulations. Periodically and as needed, this individual receives assistance from the independent authority or central office specialist(s) on requirements and inspections. This assistance may include participation in quarterly or biannual inspections. Training for the individual conducting the monthly inspections may be provided by the applicable agencies or through the agency's central office specialist(s).

The qualified departmental staff member who conducts weekly inspections of the facility may be an institutional staff member who has received training in and is familiar with the safety and sanitation requirements of the jurisdiction. At a minimum, on-the-job training from the facility's safety/sanitation specialist or the fire and safety officer regarding applicable regulations is expected, including use of checklists and methods of documentation.

The periodic weekly and monthly inspections may be conducted by either a combination of qualified individuals or one specialist, as long as the schedules and minimum qualifications described above are met. Safety and sanitation inspections may be conducted by the same person, provided this individual is familiar with the regulations for both types of inspections. When safety and sanitation requirements differ substantially, it may sometimes be necessary to call on several qualified individuals to conduct the inspections required by the standards. Using more than one person is strongly recommended.

III. COMPLIANCE AUDITS

In conducting standards compliance audits, the Commission Visiting Committees will review documentation submitted by the facilities to assist them in judging the qualifications of these individuals. In making compliance decisions, the audit teams will look closely at the facility's entire program—both practices and results—for ensuring safety and sanitation.

Appendix D

Guidelines for the Control and Use of Flammable, Toxic, and Caustic Substances (*Revised January 2001*)

This appendix provides definitions and recommendations to assist agencies in the application of standards that address the control of materials that present a hazard to staff and inmates.

Substances that do not contain any of the properties discussed in the guidelines, but are labeled "Keep out of reach of children" or "May be harmful if swallowed," are not necessarily subject to the controls specified in the guidelines. Their use and control, however, including the quantities available, should be evaluated and addressed in agency policy. Questions concerning the use and control of any substance should be resolved by examining the manufacturer's Material Safety Data Sheet.

I. DEFINITIONS

Caustic material—A substance capable of destroying or eating away by chemical reaction.

Combustible liquid—A substance with a flash point at or above 100 degrees Fahrenheit. Classified by flash point as Class II or Class III liquid.

Flammable liquid—A substance with a flash point below 100 degrees Fahrenheit (37.8 degrees Centigrade).

Flash Point—The minimum temperature at which a liquid will give off sufficient vapors to form an ignitable mixture with the air near the surface of the liquid (or in the vessel used).

Label—A written, printed, or graphic material, displayed on or affixed to containers of hazardous chemicals.

Material Safety Data Sheet (MSDS)—A document required by government regulation for all hazardous chemical substances produced and/or sold in the United States. Each MSDS sheet shall be in English and shall contain the following information: the identity used on the label, physical and chemical characteristic (vapor pressure, flash point, and so forth), physical and health hazards, primary routes of entry, exposure limits, precautions for safe handling and use, control measures, emergency and first aid procedures, and the chemical manufacturer's name, address, and telephone number.

NFPA Flammability Hazard (Red)—This degree of hazard is measured by using the flash point assigned to the product as specified on the material safety data sheet. (0, will not burn; 1, above 200F; 2, above 100 and below 200F; 3, below 100F; 4, below 73F)

NFPA Health Hazard (Blue)—The likelihood of a material to cause, either directly or indirectly, temporary or permanent injury or incapacitation due to an acute exposure by contact, inhalation, or ingestion. (0, normal material; 1, slightly hazardous; 2, moderately hazardous; 3, extreme danger; 4, deadly)

NFPA Reactivity Hazard (Yellow)—The violent chemical reaction associated with the introduction of water, chemicals also could polymerize, decompose or condense, become self-reactive, or otherwise undergo a violent chemical change under conditions of shock, pressure, or temperature. (0, stable; 1, unstable if heated; 2, violent chemical change; 3, shock and heat detonate; 4, may detonate)

NFPA Specific Hazard (White)—Other properties of the material that cause special problems or require special fire-fighting techniques (ACID=acid, ALK=alkali, COR=corrosive, OXY=oxidizer, P=polymerization, Y=radioactive).

Personal Protective Equipment (PPE)—Equipment intended to be worn by an individual to create a barrier against workplace hazards.

Secondary Container—A portable container into which chemicals are transferred for use.

Toxic Material—A substance that through which chemical reaction or mixture can produce possible injury or harm to the body by entry through the skin, digestive tract, or respiratory tract. The toxicity is dependent on the quantity absorbed and the rate, method, and the site of absorption and the concentration of the chemical.

II. PROCEDURAL GUIDELINES

Facility staff should control the use of flammable, toxic, and caustic substances through the use of a comprehensive program that begins with a review of what chemicals are in use in a particular facility. Controlling what is purchased is the critical first step in limiting the use of dangerous materials in increasing the safety and security of both staff and inmates. A thorough review process by the safety officer or other appropriate person or group can help to insure that the least dangerous product is used for a particular task. The information contained in the MSDS is critical in choosing products.

Limiting the use of extremely dangerous materials, whenever possible, is the best method of insuring the highest degree of safety for staff and inmates alike.

Diluted products with a hazardous rating (0) or (1) for health, flammability, and reactivity, using the guidelines from the MSDS, do not meet the definition of toxic material. Issue logs for these substances are not required but all containers must be labeled. MSDS sheets must be maintained on these substances and be readily available. An inventory of these products should be maintained in the primary storage area for general control purposes but is not required at the usable area.

When more dangerous materials (2, 3, or 4) must be used, a system of inventories, issue logs, and controlled storage must be instituted. At a minimum, the following areas must be addressed:

1. Stored materials must be dispensed and inventoried in accordance with written operating procedures.

2. Storage areas or cabinets must be kept inventoried and locked along with the MSDS information pertaining to the items which are contained in that area. Flammable materials must be stored in accordance with all appropriate codes and approved by the authority having jurisdiction.

3. When possible, all chemicals should be stored in their original container with the manufacturer's label intact. When chemicals are removed from the original to a secondary container, it will be labeled to identify the contents.

4. The facility safety officer or other designated person must maintain a master index of all flammable, caustic, and toxic substances used by a facility. Included with this will be all MSDS material on each substance.

5. Spills and disposal must be addressed in accordance with the guidelines indicated on the MSDS sheet.

6. A hazard communication program should be incorporated in the general staff training curriculum and a specific training program instituted for all offenders using a particular substance in either work or training activities.

7. At least annually, the control of toxic flammable and caustic chemicals should be reviewed to insure continued compliance with all aspects of the program. Any deficiencies will be addressed with remedial action.

Glossary

Absconder—a juvenile who fails to report for probation or aftercare supervision or an escapee or runaway from a juvenile placement.

Accreditation manager—an agency employee designated by the agency administrator to supervise the planning and implementation of accreditation activities in the agency. He/she has comprehensive knowledge of the agency and sufficient authority within the agency to design and administer a successful accreditation strategy.

Accreditation panel— the subunit of the Commission on Accreditation for Corrections empowered to review applications and make final decisions on agency accreditation.

Accredited status—the three-year period during which the agency maintains and improves upon its standards compliance levels that were achieved at the time of the accreditation award.

Adjudicatory hearing—a hearing to determine whether the allegations of a petition are supported by the evidence beyond a reasonable doubt or by the preponderance of the evidence.

Administrative segregation—a form of separation from the general population administered by the classification committee or other authorized group when the continued presence of the inmate in the general population would pose a serious threat to life, property, self, staff, or other inmates or to the security or orderly running of the institution. Inmates pending investigation for trial on a criminal act or pending transfer also can be included. (*See* Protective custody and Segregation.)

Administrator—*See* Program director.

Administrator of field services—the individual directly responsible for directing and controlling the operations of the adult probation and/or parole field services program. This person may be a division head in a large correctional agency, a chief probation officer answering to a judge, or the administrative officer of a court or parole authority with responsibility for the field services program.

Admission—the process of entry into a program. During admission processing, the juvenile or adult offender receives an orientation to program goals, rules, and regulations. Assignment to living quarters and to appropriate staff also is completed at this time.

Adult community residential service—also referred to as halfway house, a community-based program providing group residence (such as a house, work release center, prerelease center) for probationers, parolees, residents in incarcerated status, and referrals through the courts or other agencies. Clients also may receive these services from the agency on a nonresidential basis. (*See* Out-client.)

Adult correctional institution—a confinement facility, usually under state or federal auspices, that has custodial authority over adults sentenced to confinement for more than one year.

Adult detention facility or jail—a local confinement facility with temporary custodial authority. Adults can be confined pending adjudication for forty-eight hours or more and usually for sentences of up to two years.

Affirmative action—a concept designed to ensure equal opportunity for all persons regardless of race, religion, age, sex, or ethnic origin. These equal opportunities include all personnel programming, such as selection, promotion, retention, rate of pay, demotion, transfer, layoff, and termination.

Aftercare—control, supervision, and care exercised over juveniles released from facilities through a stated release program. (*See* Releasing authority.)

Agency—the unit of a governing authority that has direct responsibility for the operation of a corrections program, including the implementation of policy as set by the governing authority. For a community residential center, this would be the administrative headquarters of the facilities. A single community facility that is not a part of a formal consolidation of community facilities is considered to be an agency. In a public agency, this could be a probation department, welfare department, or similar agency. For a juvenile correctional organization, this would be the central office responsible for governing the juvenile correctional system for the jurisdiction.

Agency administrator—the administrative officer appointed by the governing authority or designee who is responsible for all operations of the agency, such as the department of corrections or parole, and all related programs under his or her control.

Agency industries administrator—the individual who has functional responsibility for industries operations throughout the correctional system. Titles, such as head of industries, superintendent, chief, director, or general manager, may be used to denote this position.

Alternative meal service—special foods provided to comply with the medical, religious, or security requirements. Alternative meals always must be designed to ensure that basic health needs are met and are provided in strict compliance with the policies signed by the chief executive officer, the chief medical officer, and for the religious diets, by the appropriate religious leader.

Annual certification statement—the document an accredited agency submits to ACA to verify continued compliance with the standards, report on its progress of implementing plans of action, and advise the Association of any significant events that may have occurred. It is due on the anniversary of the accreditation award.

Appeal—the agency's attempt to change the visiting committee's decision on a standard. The result of a successful appeal is a change in the status of the standard, either compliance or applicability, and a recalculation of the compliance tally.

Applicant agency—an agency involved in the exchange of materials, information, and correspondence with ACA while preparing to participate in the accreditation process.

Audit—an examination of agency or facility records or accounts to check their accuracy. It is conducted by a person or persons not directly involved in the creation and maintenance of these records or accounts. An independent audit results in an opinion that either affirms or disaffirms the accuracy of records or accounts. An operational or internal audit usually results in a report to management that is not shared with those outside the agency.

Auditor—the term frequently used to refer to ACA consultants who conduct the pre-accreditation assessments, technical assistance visits, standards compliance audits, and monitoring visits.

Authority having jurisdiction—may be a federal, state, local, or other regional department or individual, such as the fire chief, fire marshal, chief of a fire prevention bureau, labor department, health department, building official, electrical inspector, or other with standing authority who are knowledgeable about the requirements of the National Fire Protection Life Safety Code. This person may be employed by the department/agency, provided that he or she is not under the authority of the facility administrator and that the report generated is referred to higher authorities within the department/agency independent of influence by the facility administrator or staff, no matter who generates the report.

Booking—both a law enforcement process and a detention-facility procedure. As a police administrative action, it is an official recording of an arrest and the identification of the person, place, time, arresting authority, and reason for the arrest. In a detention facility, it is a procedure for the admission of a person charged with or convicted of an offense, which includes searching, fingerprinting, photographing, medical screening, and collecting personal history data. Booking also includes the inventory and storage of the individual's personal property.

Boot camp—a short-term correctional unit designed to combine elements of basic military training programs and appropriate correctional components.

Camp—a nonsecure residential program located in a relatively remote area. The residents participate in a structured program that emphasizes outdoor work, including conservation and related activities. There are often twenty to sixty residents in these facilities.

Candidate status—the period after an agency has completed its self-evaluation report. Candidate status continues until standards compliance is verified during the audit and the accreditation decision is made.

Career development plan—the planned sequence of promotions within an agency that contains provision for (1) vertical movement throughout the entire range of a particular discipline, (2) horizontal movement encouraging lateral and promotional movement among disciplines, and (3) opportunity for all to compete for the position of head of the agency. Progression along these three dimensions can occur as long as the candidate has the ambition, ability, and required qualifications.

Case conference—a conference between individuals working with the juvenile or adult offender to see that court-ordered services are being provided.

Casework—the function of the caseworker, social worker, or other professional in providing social services, such as counseling, to individuals in custody.

Caustic material—a substance capable of destroying or eating away by chemical reaction.

Cellblock—a group or cluster of single and/or multiple occupancy cells or detention rooms immediately adjacent and directly accessible to a day or activity room. In some facilities, the cellblock consists of a row of cells fronted by a dayroom of corridor-like proportions.

Chemical agent—an active substance, such as tear gas, used to defer activities that might cause personal injury or property damage.

Chemical dependency—a compulsive use of alcohol or other drugs to the point that stopping is difficult and causes physical and mental reactions.

Chief—*See* Agency industries administrator.

Chief of police—a local law enforcement official who is the appointed or elected chief executive of a police department and is responsible for the operation of the city jail or lockup.

Chronic care—health care provided to patients over a long period of time; health care services provided to patients with long-term health conditions or illnesses. Care usually includes initial assessment, treatment, and periodic monitoring to evaluate the patient's condition.

Chronic illness—a disease process or condition that persists over an extended period of time. Chronic illnesses include diabetes, hypertension, asthma, HIV, seizures, and mental health diagnosis.

Clinical services—health care services administered to offenders in a clinic setting by persons qualified to practice in one of the health care disciplines.

Clinicians—persons qualified to assess, evaluate and treat patients according to the dictates of their professional practice act. These may include physicians, nurses, physician assistants, nurse practitioners, dentists, psychologists, psychiatrists, and social workers.

Classification—a process for determining the needs and requirements of those for whom confinement has been ordered and for assigning them to housing units and programs according to their needs and existing resources.

Co-correctional facility—an institution designed to house both male and female juvenile or adult offenders.

Code of ethics—a set of rules describing acceptable standards of conduct for all employees.

Combustible liquid—a substance with a flash point at or above 100 degrees Fahrenheit, a Class II or Class III liquid.

Commission on Accreditation for Corrections (CAC)—the term used collectively to refer to the elected and appointed members empowered to render accreditation decisions.

Committing authority—the agency or court responsible for placing a juvenile in a program.

Communicable disease—a disease that can be transmitted from person to person.

Community based program—*See* Adult community residential service.

Community resources—human services agencies, service clubs, citizen interest groups, self-help groups, and individual citizen volunteers that offer services, facilities, or other functions that can meet the needs of the facility or have the potential to assist residents. These various resources, which may be public or private and national or local, may assist with material and financial support, guidance, counseling, and supportive services.

Continuity of care—health care provided on a continual basis beginning with the offender's initial contact with health care personnel and all subsequent health care encounters including referrals to community providers/facilities for offsite care during incarceration and when discharged from the institution.

Contraband—any item possessed by confined juvenile or adult offenders or found within the facility that is illegal by law or expressly prohibited by those legally charged with the administration and operation of the facility or program.

Contract—the written, signed agreement between the ACA and the agency specifying responsibilities, activities, and financial obligations.

Contractor—a person or organization that agrees to furnish materials or to perform services for the facility or jurisdiction at a specified price. Contractors operating in correctional facilities are subject to all applicable rules and regulations of the facility.

Contractual arrangement—an agreement with a private party (such as an incorporated agency or married couple) to provide services to juvenile or adult offenders for compensation. (See Independent operator.)

Control center—a very secure, self-contained unit designed to maintain the security of the facility. Policies governing the design, staffing, and accessibility of the control center ensure that it cannot be commandeered by unauthorized persons.

Controlled substance—any drug regulated by the Drug Enforcement Act.

Copayment—a fee charged an offender by the correctional institution for health care or other services.

Corporal punishment—any act of inflicting punishment directly on the body, causing pain or injury.

Correctional facility—a place used for the incarceration of individuals accused of or convicted of criminal activity. A correctional facility is managed by a single chief executive officer with broad authority for the operation of the facility. This authorization typically includes the final authority for decisions concerning (1) the employment or termination of staff members, and (2) the facility operation and programming within guidelines established by the parent agency or governing body.

A correctional facility also must have (1) a separate perimeter that precludes the regular commingling of the inmates with inmates from other facilities, (2) a separate facility budget managed by a chief executive officer within guidelines established by the parent agency or governing authority, and (3) staff that are permanently assigned to the facility.

Correspondent status—the initial period after an agency applies for accreditation. At this time, the agency evaluates its compliance with the standards and prepares a self-evaluation report.

Counseling—planned use of interpersonal relationships to promote social adjustment. Counseling programs provide opportunities to express feelings verbally with the goal of resolving the individual's problems. At least three types of counseling may be provided: individual (a one-to-one relationship), small-group counseling, and large-group counseling in a living unit.

County parole—the status of a county jail inmate who, convicted of a misdemeanor and conditionally released from a confinement facility prior to the expiration of his or her sentence, has been placed under supervision in the community for a period of time.

Credentials—documentation that demonstrates health care professionals are qualified and currently licensed, certified, and/or registered, as applicable, to provide health services within their scope of practice.

Delinquent act—an act that, if committed by an adult, would be considered a crime.

Delinquent youth—also referred to as a juvenile delinquent or a criminal-type offender, a juvenile who has been charged with or adjudicated for conduct that would, under the law of the jurisdiction in which the offense was committed, be a crime if committed by an adult. (*See also* Status offender and Juvenile.)

Dental exam—an examination by a licensed dentist that includes a dental history, exploration and charting of teeth, examination of the oral cavity, and x-rays.

Dental screen—a visual assessment of the teeth and gums by a dentist or health care staff trained by a dentist. Documentation of findings includes referrals made for dental treatment.

Detainee—any person confined in a local detention facility not serving a sentence for a criminal offense.

Detainer—a warrant placed against a person in a federal, state, or local correctional facility that notifies the holding authority of the intention of another jurisdiction to take custody of that individual when he or she is released.

Detention warrant—a warrant that authorizes the arrest and temporary detention of a parolee pending preliminary revocation proceedings. A detention warrant should be distinguished from a warrant for the return of a parolee to prison, although return warrants are sometimes used as detainers. For the purpose of these standards, return warrants used as detainers also are deemed to be detention warrants.

Detoxification—the treatment of a person who is demonstrating symptoms of intoxication or withdrawal and/or the process of gradually withdrawing alcohol or drugs from a person who is chemically dependent.

Developmental disabilities—a disorder in which there is a delay in the expected age specific development stages. These disabilities originate prior to age twenty-one, can be expected to continue indefinitely, and may constitute a substantial impairment in behavior and coping skills.

Direct supervision—a method of inmate management that ensures continuing direct contact between inmates and staff by posting an officer(s) inside each housing unit. Officers in general housing units are not separated from inmates by a physical barrier. Officers provide frequent, nonscheduled observation of and personal interaction with inmates.

Disability—a physical or mental impairment that substantially limits one or more of the major life activities of an individual; a record of such an impairment; or being regarded as having such an impairment.

Disciplinary detention—a form of separation from the general population in which inmates committing serious violations of conduct regulations are confined by the disciplinary committee or other authorized group for short periods of time to individual cells separated from the general population. Placement in detention only may occur after a finding of a rule violation at an impartial hearing and when there is not an adequate alternative disposition to regulate the inmate's behavior. (*See* Protective custody and Segregation.)

Disciplinary hearing—a nonjudicial administrative procedure to determine if substantial evidence exists to find an inmate guilty of a rule violation.

Dispositional hearing—a hearing held subsequent to the adjudicatory hearing to determine what order of disposition (for example, probation, training school, or foster home) should be made concerning a juvenile adjudicated as delinquent.

Diversion—the official halting or suspension, at any legally prescribed point after a recorded justice system entry, of formal criminal or juvenile justice proceedings against an alleged offender or juvenile. The suspension of proceedings may be in conjunction with a referral of that person to a treatment or care program administered by a nonjudicial agency or a private agency, or there may be no referral.

Due process safeguards—those procedures that ensure just, equal, and lawful treatment of an individual involved in all stages of the juvenile or criminal justice system, such as a notice of allegations, impartial and objective fact finding, the right to counsel, a written record of proceedings, a statement of any disposition ordered with the reasons for it, and the right to confront accusers, call witnesses, and present evidence.

Ectoparasites—parasites that live on the outside of the host. Examples: fleas, lice.

Education program—a program of formal academic education or a vocational training activity designed to improve employment capability.

Educational release—the designated time when residents or inmates leave the program or institution to attend school in the community and return to custody after school hours.

Emergency—any significant disruption of normal facility or agency procedure, policy, or activity caused by riot, escape, fire, natural disaster, employee action, or other serious incident.

Emergency care—care of an acute illness or unexpected health care need that cannot be deferred until the next scheduled sick call. Emergency care shall be provided to the resident population by the medical director, physician, or other staff, local ambulance services, and/or outside hospital emergency rooms. This care shall be expedited by following specific written procedures for medical emergencies described in the standards.

Environmental health—all conditions, circumstances, and surrounding influences that affect the health of individuals or groups in the area.

Expected practices—actions and activities that if implemented properly (according to protocols) will produce the desired outcome. They are what we think is necessary to achieve and maintain compliance with the standard—but not necessarily the only way to do so. They are activities that represent the current experience of the field, but that are not necessarily supported by research. As the field learns and evolves, so will the practices.

Facility—a place, institution, building (or part thereof), set of buildings, or area (whether or not enclosing a building or set of buildings) that is used for the lawful custody and/or treatment of individuals. It may be owned and/or operated by public or private agencies and includes the staff and services as well as the buildings and grounds.

Facility administrator—any official, regardless of local title (for example sheriff, chief of police, administrator, warden/superintendent) who has the ultimate responsibility for managing and operating the facility.

Field agency—the unit of a governing authority that has direct responsibility for the provision of field supervision services and for the carrying out of policy as set by the governing authority.

Field services—services provided to delinquent juveniles, status offenders, or adult offenders in the community by probation, parole, or other agencies.

Field staff/field workers—the professionals assigned case responsibility for control, supervision, and provision of program services to delinquent juveniles or adult offenders.

First aid—care for a condition that requires immediate assistance from an individual trained in first aid care and the use of the facility's first aid kits.

Fiscal position control—the process that ensures that individuals on the payroll are legally employed, positions are authorized in the budget, and funds are available.

Flammable liquid—a substance with a flash point below 100 degrees Fahrenheit, classified as a Class I liquid.

Flash point—the minimum temperature at which a liquid will give off sufficient vapors to form an ignitable mixture with the air near the surface of the liquid (or in the vessel used).

Footcandle—a unit for measuring the intensity of illumination, defined as the amount of light thrown on a surface one foot away from the light source.

Formulary—a list of prescription and nonprescription medications that have been approved by the health authority and are stocked or routinely procured for use in an institution.

Furlough/Temporary leave—a period of time during which a resident is allowed to leave the facility and go into the community unsupervised.

Goal statement—a general statement of what is sought within the functional area of the performance-based standard.

Good-time—a system established by law whereby a convicted offender is credited a set amount of time, which is subtracted from his or her sentence, for specified periods of time served in an acceptable manner.

Governing authority—in public/governmental agencies, the administrative department or division to which the agency reports; the policy-setting body. In private agencies, this may be an administrative headquarters, central unit, or the board of directors or trustees.

Grievance/Grievance process—a circumstance or action considered to be unjust and grounds for complaint or resentment and/or a response to that circumstance in the form of a written complaint filed with the appropriate body.

Halfway house—*See* Adult community residential service.

Handicapped—having a mental or physical impediment or disadvantage that substantially limits an individual's ability to use programs or services.

Head of industries—*See* Agency industries administrator.

Health agency—an organization that provides health care services to an institution or a system of institutions.

Health appraisal—the physician, health administrator, or agency-designated individual responsible for the coordination and management of health services within an institution.

Health authority—the health administrator, or agency responsible for the provision of health care services at an institution or system of institutions; the responsible physician may be the health authority.

Health care—the sum of all action taken, preventative and therapeutic, to provide for the physical and mental well-being of a population. It includes medical and dental services, mental health services, nursing, personal hygiene, dietary services, and environmental conditions.

Health care personnel—individuals whose primary duty is to provide health services to inmates in keeping with their respective levels of health care training or experience.

Health care provider—an individual licensed in the delivery of health care.

Health care services—a system of preventative and therapeutic services that provide for the physical and mental well-being of a population. Includes medical and dental services, mental health services, nursing, pharmaceutical services, personal hygiene, dietary services, and environmental conditions.

Health/medical screen—a structured inquiry and observation to prevent newly arrived offenders who pose a health or safety threat to themselves or others from being admitted to the general population and to identify offenders who require immediate medical attention. The screen can be initiated at the time of admission by health care personnel or by a health trained correctional officer.

Health-trained personnel/Medically trained personnel—correctional officers or other correctional personnel who may be trained and appropriately supervised to carry out specific duties with regard to the administration of health care.

Hearing—a proceeding to determine a course of action, such as the placement of a juvenile or adult offender, or to determine guilt or innocence in a disciplinary matter. Argument, witnesses, or evidence are heard by a judicial officer or administrative body in making the determination.

Hearing examiner—an individual appointed by the parole authority who conducts hearings for the authority. His or her power of decision making may include, but not be limited to, making parole recommendations to granting, denying, or revoking parole.

Holding facility/Lockup—a temporary confinement facility, for which the custodial authority is usually less than forty-eight hours, where arrested persons are held pending release, adjudication, or transfer to another facility.

Holidays—all days legally designated as nonworkdays by statute or by the chief governing authority of a jurisdiction.

House parent—*See* Program director.

Improvement—*See* Quality assurance.

Independent operator—a person or persons who contract with a correctional agency or other governmental agency to operate and manage a correctional program or facility.

Independent outside source—*See* Authority having jurisdiction.

Independent source—a person, organization or group that acts independently from the correctional unit being evaluated. An independent source may not be a staff member who reports to the chief executive officer of the unit being audited.

Indigent—an individual with no funds or source of income.

Industries—an activity existing in a correctional system that uses inmate labor to produce goods and/or services for sale. These goods and/or services are sold at prices calculated to recover all or a substantial portion of costs associated with their production and may include a margin of profit. Sale of the products and/or services is not limited to the institution where the industries activity is located.

Infection control program—a program designed to investigate, prevent, and control the spread of infections and communicable disease.

Infirmary—a specific area within an institution, separate from other housing areas, where offenders are admitted for health observation and care under the supervision and direction of health care personnel.

Information system/Management information system—the concepts, personnel, and supporting technology for the collection, organization, and delivery of information for administrative use. There are two such types of information: (1) standard information, consisting of the data required for operations control such as the daily count, payroll data in a personnel office, probation/parole success rates, referral sources, and caseload levels; (2) demand information, consisting of information that can be generated when a report is required, such as information on the number of residents in educational and training programs, duration of residence, or the number of residents eligible for discharge during a twelve-month period by offense, sentence, and month of release.

Informed consent—the agreement by a patient to a treatment, examination, or procedure after the patient receives the material facts regarding the nature, consequences, risks, and alternatives concerning the proposed treatment, examination, or procedure.

Inmate—any individual, whether in pretrial, unsentenced, or sentenced status, who is confined in a correctional facility.

Institution industries manager—the individual designated as responsible for industries operations at a specific institution in the correctional system.

Interstate compact on juveniles—an agreement authorizing the interstate supervision of juvenile delinquents. This can also include the cooperative institutionalization of special types of delinquent juveniles, such as psychotics and special needs delinquents.

Interstate compact for the supervision of probationers and parolees—an agreement entered into by eligible jurisdictions in the United States and its territories that provides the criteria for these jurisdictions to cooperate in working with probation and release.

Jail—*See* Adult detention facility.

Judicial review—a proceeding to reexamine the course of action or continued confinement of a juvenile in a secure detention facility. Arguments, witnesses, or evidence are not required as part of the review. Reviews may be conducted by a judge, judicial officer, or an administrator who has been delegated the authority to release juveniles from secure detention with the approval of the judge.

Juvenile—a person under the age of twenty-one, or as defined in the local jurisdiction as under the age of majority.

Juvenile community residential program—a program housed in a structure without security fences and security hardware or other major restraining construction typically associated with correctional facilities, such as a converted apartment building or private home. They are not constructed as or intended to be detention facilities. Except for daycare programs, they provide twenty-four-hour care, programs, and supervision to juveniles in residence. Their focus is on providing the juvenile with positive adult models and program activities that assist in resolving problems specific to this age group in an environment conducive to positive behavior in the community.

Juvenile correction center—*See* Training school.

Juvenile day treatment program—a program that provides services to juveniles who live at home and report to the program on a daily basis. Juveniles in these programs require more attention than that provided by probation and aftercare services. Often the program operates its own education program through the local school district. The population usually is drawn from court commitments but may include juveniles enrolled as a preventive or diversionary measure. The program may operate as part of a residential program, and it may provide space for occasional overnight stays by program participants where circumstances warrant additional assistance.

Juvenile delinquent—*See* delinquent youth.

Juvenile detention—temporary care of juvenile offenders and juveniles alleged to be delinquent who require secure custody in a physically restricting facility.

Juvenile development center—*See* Juvenile correctional facility.

Juvenile group home—nonsecure residential program emphasizing family-style living in a homelike atmosphere. Program goals are similar to those for large community residential programs. Although group homes usually house juveniles who are court-committed, they also house abused or neglected juveniles who are placed by social agencies. Small group homes serve from four to eight juveniles; large group homes serve eight-to-twelve. Participating juveniles range in age from 10 to 17, with the concentration from 13 to 16.

Juvenile intake—process of determining whether the interests of the public or the juvenile require the filing of a petition with the juvenile court. Generally, an intake officer receives, reviews, and processes complaints, recommends detention or release, and provides services for juveniles and their families, including diversion and referral to other community agencies.

Juvenile nonresidential program—a program that provides services to juveniles who live at home and report to the program on a daily basis. Juveniles in these programs require more attention than that provided by probation and aftercare services. Often the program operates its own education program through the local school district. The population of non-residential programs may be as many as 50 boys and girls ranging in age from 10 to 18. The population is usually drawn from court commitments but may include juveniles enrolled as a preventive or diversionary measure. The program may operate as part of a residential program, and it may provide space for occasional overnight stays by program participants where circumstances warrant additional assistance.

Juvenile ranch—nonsecure residential program providing services to juveniles in a rural setting. Typically, the residents participate in a structured program of education, recreation, and facility maintenance, including responsibility for the physical plant, its equipment, and livestock. Often there are 20-to-60 juveniles in the ranch setting, ranging in age from 13-to-18.

Juvenile service center—*See* Juvenile correctional facility.

Juvenile village—*See* Juvenile correctional facility.

Library service—a service that provides reading materials for convenient use; circulation of reading materials; service to help provide users with library materials, educational and recreational audio/visual materials, or a combination of these services.

Life Safety Code—a manual published and updated by the National Fire Protection Association specifying minimum standards for fire safety necessary in the public interest. Two chapters are devoted to correctional facilities.

Lockup—*See* Holding facility.

Mail inspection—examination of incoming and outgoing mail for contraband, cash, checks, and money orders.

Major equipment—equipment that is securely and permanently fastened to the building or any equipment with a current book value of $1,000 or more.

Major infraction—rule violation involving a grievous loss and requiring imposition of due process procedures. Major infractions include (1) violations that may result in disciplinary detention or administrative segregation; (2) violations for which punishment may tend to increase an inmate's sentence; (3) violations that may result in a forfeiture, such as loss of good-time or work time; and (4) violations that may be referred for criminal prosecution.

Mandatory standard—a standard that has been determined by the American Correctional Association to directly affect the life, health, and safety of offenders and correctional personnel.

Management information system—*See* Information system.

Master index file—used in an institution to keep track of the inmates who are housed in particular housing units.

Medical records—separate records of medical examinations and diagnoses maintained by the responsible physician. The date and time of all medical examinations and copies of standing or direct medical orders from the physician to the facility staff should be transferred to the resident's record.

Medical restraints—chemical restraints, such as sedatives, or physical restraints, such as straitjackets, applied only for medical or psychiatric purposes. Metal handcuffs and leg shackles are not considered medical restraints.

Medical screen—*See* Health screen.

Medically trained personnel—*See* Health trained personnel.

Medication administration—process of giving a dose of a prescribed or over-the-counter medication to a patient.

Medication dispensing—the process of placing one or more doses of a medication into a container that is labeled to indicate the name of the patient, the contents of the container, and other necessary information by health care staff member as authorized by the jurisdiction.

Medication disposal—destruction or removal of medication from a facility after discontinuation of its use per local, state, and federal regulation.

Mental health care practitioner—staff who perform clinical duties for mentally ill patients, for example, physicians, psychologists, nurses, and social workers in accordance with each health care professional's scope of training and applicable licensing, certification, and regulatory requirements.

Mental health screening—review by a qualified, mental health professional of any history of psychological problems and examination of any current psychological problems to determine, with reasonable assurances, that the individual poses no significant risk to themselves or others.

Mental health staff—individuals whose primary duty is to provide mental health services to inmates commensurate with their respective levels of education, experience, training, and credentials.

Mental illness—psychiatric illness or disease expressed primarily through abnormalities of thought, feeling, and behavior producing either distress and/or impaired function.

Mental retardation—developmental disability marked by lower-than-normal intelligence and impaired daily living skills.

Mid-level practitioner—nurse practitioner or physician assistant licensed or credentialed to assume an expanded role in providing medical care under the supervision of a physician.

Minor infraction—a violation of the facility's rules of conduct that does not require due process and can be resolved without the imposition of serious penalties. Minor infractions do not violate any state or federal statutes and may be resolved informally by the reporting staff.

Natural light—the illumination from the sun; daylight.

NFPA—National Fire Protection Association, which publishes the *Life Safety Code*.

National uniform parole reports system—cooperative effort sponsored by the National Parole Institute that calls for the voluntary cooperation of all federal and state authorities having responsibility for felony offenders in developing some common terms to describe parolee (age, sex, and prior record) and some common definitions to describe parole performance. These types of data allow comparisons across states and other jurisdictions.

Non-applicable—term used in the accreditation process to describe a standard that does not apply to the correctional unit being audited. While the initial determination of applicability is made by American Correctional Association staff and/or the audit team, the final decision rests with the Commission on Accreditation.

Noncontact visiting—a program that restricts inmates from having physical contact with visitors. Physical barriers usually separate the offender from the visitors with screens and/or glass. Voice communications between the parties are typically accomplished with phones or speakers. Offenders who present a serious escape threat, are a threat to others, or require protection are often designated for noncontact visits.

Non-formulary medication—medications not listed in the approved institution or agency formulary.

Occupational exposure—exposure to potentially harmful chemical, physical, or biological agents that occur as a result of one's occupation.

Offender—individual convicted or adjudicated of a criminal offense.

Official personnel file—current and accurate record of the employee's job history, including all pertinent information relating to that history.

Operating unit—one distinct operation of the industry's activity, which may be operated as a cost center or separate accounting entity. It may take the form of a manufacturing operation (for example, furniture making or clothing production), an agricultural operation (for example, dairy or poultry farming, crop or orchard farming, cow or pig farming), or a service activity (for example, a warehouse, keypunch operation, microfilming process, laundering, auto repair, and so forth).

Orientation and reception—the reception period includes interviews, testing, and other admissions-related activities; including distribution of information about programs, services, rules, and regulations.

Out-client—individual who does not live at the facility but who may use facility services and programs.

Outcome measure—measurable events, occurrences, conditions, behaviors, or attitudes that demonstrate the extent to which a condition described has been achieved.

Parent—individual with whom a juvenile regularly lives and who is the biological, adoptive, or surrogate parent.

Parent agency—administrative department or division to whom the agency seeking accreditation reports; the policy-setting body.

Parole authority/Parole board/Parole commission—decision-making body that has responsibility to grant, deny, and/or revoke parole. The term "parole authority" includes all of these bodies.

Parole hearing—procedure conducted by a parole authority member and/or hearing examiner in which all pertinent aspects of an eligible inmate's case are reviewed to make a decision or recommendation that would change the inmate's legal status and/or degree of freedom.

Peer review—process of having patient care provided by a clinician reviewed and evaluated by a peer with similar credentials. An external peer review is completed by a medical professional not employed by the facility being reviewed.

Perimeter security—a system that controls ingress and egress to the interior of a facility or institution. The system may include electronic devices, walls, fences, patrols, and/or towers.

Permanent status—personnel status that provides due process protection prior to dismissal.

Personal property—property that legally belongs to the offender.

Personnel policies manual—a manual that is available to each employee and contains the following: an affirmative action program, an equal opportunity program, a policy for selection, retention, and promotion of all personnel on the basis of merit and specified qualifications, a code of ethics, rules for probationary employment, a compensation and benefit plan, provisions of the Americans with Disabilities Act (ADA), sexual harassment and sexual misconduct policy, grievance and appeal procedures, infection control procedures, and employees disciplinary procedures.

Petition—application for a court order or other judicial action. For example, a delinquency petition is an application for the court to act in the matter of a juvenile apprehended for a delinquent act.

Physical examination—evaluation of a patient's current physical condition and medical history conducted by or under the supervision of a licensed professional.

Placing authority—agency or body with the authority to order a juvenile into a specific dispositional placement. This may be the juvenile court, the probation department, or another duly constituted and authorized placement agency.

Policy—course or line of action adopted and pursued by an agency that guides and determines present and future decisions and actions. Policies indicate the general course or direction of an organization within which the activities of the personnel must operate. They are statements of guiding principles that should be followed in directing activities toward the attainment of objectives. Attainment may lead to compliance with standards and compliance with the overall goals of the agency or system.

Population center—geographical area containing at least 10,000 people, along with public safety services, professional services, employment and educational opportunities, and cultural/recreational opportunities.

Preliminary hearing—hearing to determine whether probable cause exists to support an allegation of parole violation pending a revocation hearing by the parole authority.

Pretrial release—procedure whereby an accused individual who had been taken into custody is allowed to be released before and during his or her trial.

Preventive maintenance—a system designed to enhance the longevity and or usefulness of buildings or equipment in accordance with a planned schedule.

Private agency—the contracting agency of the governing authority that has direct responsibility for the operation of a corrections program.

Probation—court-ordered disposition alternative through which a convicted adult offender or an adjudicated delinquent is placed under the control, supervision, and care of a probation field staff member.

Probationary period—a period of time designated to evaluate and test an employee to ascertain fitness for the job.

Procedure—detailed and sequential actions that must be executed to ensure that a policy is fully implemented. It is the method of performing an operation or a manner of proceeding on a course of action. It differs from a policy in that it directs action in a particular situation to perform a specific task within the guidelines of policy.

Process indicators—documentation and other evidence that can be examined periodically and continuously to determine that practices are being properly implemented.

Professional association—collective body of individuals engaged in a particular profession or vocation.

Professional staff—social workers, probation officers, and other staff assigned to juvenile and adult offender cases. These individuals generally possess bachelor's degrees and advanced training in the social or behavioral sciences.

Program—plan or system through which a correctional agency works to meet its goals. This program may require a distinct physical setting, such as a correctional institution, community residential facility, group home, or foster home.

Program director—individual directly in charge of the program.

Prosthesis—functional or cosmetic artificial device that substitutes for a missing body part such as an arm, leg, eye, or tooth.

Protective custody—form of separation from the general population for inmates requesting or requiring protection from other inmates for reasons of health or safety. The inmate's status is reviewed periodically by the classification committee or other designated group. (*See* Administrative segregation and Disciplinary detention.)

Protocols—written instructions that guide implementation of expected practices, such as policies and procedures, training curriculum, offender handbooks, diagrams, and internal forms and logs.

Psychotropic medication—medication that exerts an effect on thought, mood, and/or behavior. Psychotropic medications are used to treat mental illness and a variety of disorders.

Public agency—the governing authority that has direct responsibility for the operation of a corrections program.

Qualified medical person—*See* Health care professional.

Qualified mental health person—*See* Mental health care practitioner.

Quality assurance—formal, internal monitoring program that uses standardized criteria to insure quality and consistency. The program identifies opportunities for improvement, develops improvement strategies, and monitors effectiveness.

Rated capacity—the original architectural design plus, or minus, capacity changes resulting from building additions, reductions, or revisions.

Reasonable accommodation—modifications or adjustments, which enable qualified applicants with disabilities to access the job application process or which enable qualified employees with disabilities to perform the essential functions of the job and to enjoy the same terms, conditions, and privileges of employment that are available to persons without disabilities.

Reasonably private environment—this may vary, depending on individual and institutional circumstances, but it is one which will maintain the dignity of the disabled individual in light of that person's disability

Records (juvenile and adult offenders)—information concerning the individual's delinquent or criminal, personal and medical history and behavior, and activities while in custody, including but not limited to commitment papers, court orders, detainers, personal property receipts, visitors' lists, photographs, fingerprints, type of custody, disciplinary infractions and actions taken, grievance reports, work assignments, program participation, and miscellaneous correspondence.

Referral—process by which a juvenile or adult offender is introduced to an agency or service that can provide the needed assistance.

Release on bail—release by a judicial officer of an accused individual who has been taken into custody on the accused's promise to appear in court as required for criminal proceedings.

Releasing authority—decision-making body and/or individual who has the authority to grant, deny, and revoke release from a juvenile institution or program of supervision. In some jurisdictions, it is called the parole board or the parole commission.

Renovation—significant structural or design change in the physical plant of a facility.

Responsible physician—individual licensed to practice medicine and provide health services to the inmate population of the facility and/or the physician at an institution with final responsibility for decisions related to medical judgments.

Restraints—devices used to restrict physical activity; for example, handcuffs, leg irons, straight-jackets, belly chain.

Revocation hearing—hearing before the parole authority to determine whether revocation of parole should be made final.

Rule book, offender—a collection of the facility's rules of conduct and sanctions for violations defined in writing.

Safety equipment—primarily firefighting equipment, such as chemical extinguishers, hoses, nozzles, water supplies, alarm systems, sprinkler systems, portable breathing devices, gas masks, fans, first aid kits, stretchers, and emergency alarms.

Safety vestibule—grille cage that divides the inmate areas from the remainder of the institution. They must have two doors or gates, only one of which opens at a time, to permit entry to or exit from inmate areas in a safe and controlled manner.

Sallyport—enclosure situated in the perimeter wall or fence of a correctional facility containing gates or doors at both ends, only one of which opens at a time, ensuring there will be no breach in the perimeter security of the institution. The sallyport may handle either pedestrian or vehicular traffic.

School or home for boys and girls—*See* Juvenile correctional facility.

Secure institution—facility that is designed and operated to ensure that all entrances and exits are under the exclusive control of the facility's staff preventing an inmate/resident from leaving the facility unsupervised or without permission.

Security devices—locks, gates, doors, bars, fences, screens, ceilings, floors, walls, and barriers used to confine and control detained individuals. Also included are electronic monitoring equipment, security alarm systems, security lights, auxiliary power supplies, and other equipment used to maintain facility security.

Security perimeter—outer portions of a facility that provide for secure confinement of facility inmates/residents. The design of the perimeter may vary dependent on the security classification of the facility.

Segregation—confinement of an inmate to an individual cell separated from the general population. There are three forms of segregation: administrative segregation, disciplinary detention, and protective custody.

Segregation unit—a housing section that separates offenders who threaten the security or orderly management of the institution from the general population.

Self-insurance coverage—system designed to insure the payment of all legal claims for injury or damage incurred as a result of the actions of state officials, employees, or agents. In public agencies, the self-insurance program is usually authorized by the legislature. A "memorandum of insurance" or similar document is required that acts as a policy, setting the limits of liability for various categories of risk, including deductible limits. Approval of the policy by a cabinet-level official is also required.

Serious incident—situation in which injury serious enough to warrant medical attention occurs involving a resident, employee, or visitor on the grounds of the institution. A situation creating an imminent threat to the security of the institution and/or to the safety of residents, employees, or visitors on the grounds of the institution.

Severe mental disturbance—condition in which an individual is a danger to self or others or is incapable of attending to basic physiological needs.

Shelter facility—non-secure public or private facility designated to provide either temporary placement for alleged or adjudicated status offenders prior to the issuance of a disposition order or longer-term care under a juvenile court disposition order.

Special management inmates—individuals whose behavior presents a serious threat to the safety and security of the facility, staff, general inmate population, or themselves. Special handling and/or housing is required to regulate their behavior.

Special needs—mental and/or physical condition that requires accommodations or arrangements differing from those a general population offender or juvenile normally would receive. Offenders or juveniles with special needs may include, but are not limited to, the emotionally disturbed, developmentally disabled, mentally ill, physically handicapped, chronically ill, the disabled or infirm, and the drug or alcohol addicted.

Standard—statement that defines a required or essential condition to be achieved and/or maintained.

Status offender—juvenile who has been charged with or adjudicated for conduct that under the law of the jurisdiction in which the offense was committed would not be a crime if committed by an adult. (See also Delinquent youth.)

Strip search—examination of an inmate's/resident's naked body for weapons, contraband, and physical abnormalities. This also includes a thorough search of all of the individual's clothing while it is not being worn.

Superintendent—See Warden.

Temporary disability—a condition that can be treated with an expectation of full recovery. They are not the result of chronic conditions, are short-term in nature and resolve over time.

Temporary leave—*See* Furlough.

Temporary release—period of time during which an inmate is allowed to leave the program or institution and go into the community unsupervised for various purposes consistent with the public interest.

Terms, conditions, privileges of employment—include, but are not limited to: recruitment, selection, and hiring; salary and compensation; benefits, holidays, leave, and work hours; promotion and advancement; staff development, including in-service training; and retirement, resignation, and termination

Therapeutic community—a designed social environment with programs for substance-use-disordered patients within a residential or day unit in which the social and group process is used with therapeutic intent.

Therapeutic diet—diet prescribed by a health care practitioner as part of the patient's medical treatment. Therapeutic diets can be ordered by physicians, physician's assistants, or nurse practitioners.

Training—an organized, planned, documented, and evaluated or assessed activity designed to impart knowledge and skills to enhance job performance. Training is based on specific objectives, is job related, from an appropriate source, of sufficient duration, relevant to organizational need, and delivered to appropriate staff.

Elements of Defendable Training:

1. Based upon specific objectives.
    Performance objectives (intent of training)
    Formal lesson plans or functional equivalent (content of training)
2. Must be job-related
    Job analysis (new employee)
    Need resulting from problem analysis (existing employee)
3. From an appropriate source
    Qualified by credentials
    Qualified by knowledge and/or skills
    Qualified by performance
    "Delivery Skills Qualified"
4. Of sufficient duration (quantity of training)
    Hours–how long did it take to learn?
    Must be reasonably related to the complexity/importance of the topic
5. Where something relevant is learned (quality of training)
    Student feedback
    Student evaluation and proficiency testing
    Improved performance on the job
    Agency improvements
6. Appropriate staff were attending
    Topics related to job tasks and/or performance problems
    Attendance documented with name roster and title/positions of staff that perform tasks or share problems

Training plan—a set of long or short range training activities that equip staff with the knowledge, skills, and attitudes that they need to accomplish the goals of the agency.

Training school—*See* Juvenile correctional facility.

Treatment plan—series of written statements that specify the particular course of therapy and the roles of medical and nonmedical personnel in carrying it out. A treatment plan is individualized, based on assessment of the individual patient's needs, and includes a statement of the short- and long-term goals and the methods by which the goals will be pursued. When clinically indicated, the treatment plan provides inmates with access to a range of supportive and rehabilitative services, such as individual or group counseling and/or self-help groups that the physician deems appropriate.

Triage—screening and classification of offender health care concerns by qualified medical staff to determine the priority of need and the appropriate level of intervention.

Undue hardship—an accommodation that would be unduly costly, extensive, or substantial.

Unencumbered space—Usable space that is not encumbered by furnishings or fixtures. At least one dimension of the unencumbered space is no less than seven feet. In determining unencumbered space in the area, the total square footage is obtained and the square footage of fixtures and equipment is subtracted. All fixtures and equipment must be in operational position.

Unit management—Management system that subdivides an institution into units. The unit management system has several basic requirements:

1. Each unit holds a relatively small number of inmates. Ideally, there should be fewer than 150 but not more than 500 inmates.
2. Inmates are housed in the same unit for a major portion of their confinement.
3. Inmates assigned to a unit work in a close relationship with a multidisciplinary staff team who are regularly assigned to the unit and whose officers are located within the unit.
4. Staff members have decision-making authority for the institutional programming and living conditions for the inmates assigned to the unit within broad rules, policies, and guidelines established by the agency and/or the facility administrator.
5. Inmate assignments to a unit are based on the inmate's need for control, security, and programs offered.

Unit management increases contact between staff and inmates, fosters increased interpersonal relationships, and leads to more knowledgeable decision making as a direct result of staff dealing with a smaller, more permanent group. At the same time, the facility benefits from the economies inherent in centralized service facilities, such as utilities, food service, health care, educational systems, vocational programs, and recreational facilities.

Urine surveillance program—program whereby urine samples are collected on an irregular basis from offenders suspected of having a history of drug use to determine current or recent use.

Use of force—refers to the right of an individual or authority to settle conflicts or prevent certain actions by applying measures to either dissuade another party from a particular course of action, or physically intervene to stop them. The use of force is governed by statute and is usually authorized in a progressive series of actions, referred to as a "use-of-force continuum."

Volunteer—individual who donates his or her time and effort to enhance the activities and programs of the agency. They are selected on the basis of their skills or personal qualities to provide services in recreation, counseling, education, religion, and so forth.

Warden—individual in charge of the institution; the chief executive or administrative officer. This position is sometimes referred to by other titles, but "warden" and "superintendent" are the most commonly used terms.

Work release—formal arrangement sanctioned by law whereby an inmate/resident is released into the community to maintain approved and regular employment.

Workers' compensation—statewide system of benefits for employees who are disabled by job-related injury.

Work stoppage—a planned or spontaneous discontinuation of work. The stoppage may involve employees or inmates, acting separately or in concert by refusing to participate in institutional activities.

Youthful offender—person under the age of criminal majority in the jurisdiction in which he or she is confined.

Introduction to Certification and Accreditation

For jails that are interested in securing an independent assessment of compliance with these standards, the American Correctional Association (ACA) and the Commission on Accreditation for Corrections (CAC) offer a new "certification" process. Certification is similar in scope and practice to ACA's longstanding accreditation process. Certification involves a site visit by one or more professional auditors who determine compliance with each of the standards and expected practices. Accreditation is available for agencies that wish to comply with the full set of Performance-Based Standards for Adult Local Detention Facilities (ALDF).

ACA and CAC are private, nonprofit organizations that administer the only national accreditation and certification programs for all components of adult and juvenile corrections. Their purpose is to promote improvement in the management of correctional agencies through the administration of a voluntary accreditation program and the ongoing development and revision of relevant, useful standards. The accreditation process began in 1978 and certification for core jail standards was introduced in 2010. Certification offers the opportunity to evaluate operations against national minimum jail standards, remedy deficiencies, and upgrade the quality of correctional programs and services. The recognized benefits from such a process include improved management, a defense against lawsuits through documentation and the demonstration of a "good faith" effort to improve conditions of confinement, increased accountability and enhanced public credibility for administrative and line staff, a safer and more humane environment for personnel and offenders, and the establishment of measurable criteria for upgrading programs, personnel, and the physical plant on a continuing basis.

The timelines, requirements, and outcomes of the certification process are the same as those that are provided for the ALDF standards and for other criminal justice agencies, such as state or federal prisons, training schools, local detention facilities, private halfway houses or group homes, probation and parole field service agencies, or paroling authorities. A jail that wants to be certified signs a contract with ACA, pays a certification fee, conducts a self-evaluation, and has an onsite standards compliance audit by trained ACA auditors. The final certification decision is made by the Commission on Accreditation for Corrections. Once certified, the jail must submit annual reports and statements to ACA. Also, at ACA's expense and discretion, a monitoring visit may be conducted during the initial three-year certification period to ensure continued compliance with the appropriate standards.

Participation in the Certification Process

Any interested agency that operates a jail is invited to participate in the certification process. Participating agencies may include public and private agencies and federal, state, and local agencies. Certification activities are initiated voluntarily by correctional administrators. When an agency chooses to pursue certification, ACA staff will provide the agency with appropriate information and application materials. These include a contract, the applicable manual of standards, a policy and procedure manual, and an organization summary.

Eligibility Criteria

To be eligible for certification, an agency must be a part of a governmental or private entity or conform to the applicable federal, state, or local laws and regulations regarding corporate existence. The agency must: (1) hold under confinement pretrial or presentenced adults or juveniles who are being held pending a hearing for unlawful activity; or (2) hold under confinement sentenced adult offenders convicted of criminal activity or juveniles adjudicated to confinement; and (3) have a single administrative officer responsible for agency operations. It is this administrative officer who makes the formal application for admission for certification.

It is ACA's policy that nonadjudicated juveniles should be served outside the juvenile correctional system. Detention facilities may house status offenders who have violated valid court orders by continued perpetration of status offenses. In such instances, the following conditions would apply: status offenders are separated by sight and sound from delinquent offenders; facility staffs demonstrate attempts to mandate removal of all status offenders from detention centers; and special programs are developed for status offenders.

Pre-Certification Assessment

Prior to signing a certification contract, an agency may request a pre-certification assessment. The assessment involves an ACA auditor visiting the agency. The auditor will assess strengths and areas for improvement, measure readiness for the application for certification, and identify steps required to achieve certification. A confidential, written report is provided to the agency to assist in making the decision to apply for certification. A pre-certification assessment is not required.

Applicant Status

When the agency enters into the certification process, the administrator requests an information package from ACA. To confirm eligibility, determine appropriate fees, and schedule certification activities, the agency provides ACA with relevant narrative information through the organization summary. Applicant Status begins when both the completed organization summary, which provides a written description of the facility/program and the signed contract are returned to ACA. The Association will notify the agency of its acceptance into the certification process within fifteen days of the receipt of the necessary application materials. ACA will then assign a staff member from the Standards and Accreditation Department as a permanent liaison to the agency. The agency will appoint a certification manager, who will be responsible for organizing and supervising agency resources and activities to achieve certification.

As defined in the contract, the fees for the certification period cover all services normally provided to an agency by ACA staff, auditors, and the Commission. The fees are determined during the application period and are included in the contract signed by the agency and ACA.

Correspondent Status

When the application is accepted, the agency enters into Correspondent Status. During this time, the agency conducts a self-assessment of its operations and completes a self-evaluation report, which specifies the agency's level of standards compliance. (Self-evaluation reports are optional for facilities signing a recertification contract.)

At the agency's request and expense, an on-site certification orientation for staff and/or a field consultation may be scheduled. The object of the orientation is to prepare agency staff to complete the requirements of certification, including an understanding of self-evaluation activities, compilation of documentation, audit procedures, and standards interpretation. A field auditor provides information on certification policy and procedure, standards interpretations, and/or documentation requirements. Agency familiarity with standards and certification is the key factor in determining the need for these services.

The self-evaluation report includes the organizational summary, a compliance tally, preliminary requests for waivers or plans of action, and a completed standards compliance checklist for each standard in the applicable manual.

Applicable Standards

The standards used for certification address services, programs, and operations essential to good correctional management, including administrative, staff, and fiscal controls, staff training and development, physical plant, safety and emergency procedures, sanitation, food service, rules and discipline, and a variety of subjects that comprise good correctional practice. These standards are under continual revision to reflect changing practice, current case law, new knowledge, and agency experience with their application. These changes are published by ACA in the *Standards Supplement.*

ACA policy addresses the impact of the standards revisions on agencies involved in certification. Agencies signing contracts after the date that a *Standards Supplement* is published are held accountable for all standards changes in that supplement. Agencies are not held accountable for changes made after the contract is signed. The agencies may choose to apply new changes to the standards that have been issued following the program's entry into certification. Agencies must notify ACA of their decision before conducting the standards compliance audit.

For certification purposes, any new architectural design, building, and/or renovation of the institution must be in accordance with the current standards manual at the time of the design, building, and/or renovation. In such cases, different standards would be applied to separate parts of the institution, respective to these changes in the physical plant.

Standards Compliance Checklist

In completing a standards compliance checklist, the agency checks compliance, noncompliance, or not applicable for each standard. Checking compliance signifies complete compliance with the content of the standard at all times and that the agency has documentation (primarily written) available to support compliance. A finding of noncompliance indicates that all or part of the requirements stated in the standard have not been met. A not applicable response means that the standard/expected practice is clearly not relevant to the agency/facility being audited. A written statement supporting nonapplicability of the standard/expected practice is required.

At this time, the agency may request a waiver for one or more standards, provided that overall agency programming compensates for the lack of compliance. The waiver request must be accompanied by a clear explanation of the compensating conditions. The agency applies for a waiver only when the totality of conditions safeguard the life, health, and safety of offenders and staff. Waivers are not granted for standards/expected practices designated as mandatory and do not change the conclusion of noncompliance or the agency's compliance tally. When a waiver is requested during the self-evaluation phase, ACA staff renders a preliminary judgment. A final decision can be made only by the Board of Commissioners during the certification hearing.

Most waivers granted are for physical plant standards. The Association requires that a self-evaluation report be completed by each applicant for certification. It is recommended that agencies entering into the certification process for the first time submit a written statement to ACA concerning their status at the completion of the evaluation. Information contained in this statement should include the percentage of compliance with mandatory and nonmandatory standards; a list of not applicable standards/expected practices; and a list of noncompliant standards and their deficiencies. Within sixty days of receipt of this statement, ACA staff will provide the agency administrator with a written response containing, where appropriate, comments on materials or information submitted to the Association.

The letter also provides notice to the agency of its acceptance to Candidate Status. The compilation of written documentation requires the most time and effort during Correspondent Status. A separate documentation file, which documents compliance, is prepared for each standard. To request an audit, an agency must comply with 100 percent of the standards/expected practices designated as mandatory and 90 percent of the nonmandatory standards/expected practices.

Candidate Status

The agency enters into Candidate Status with ACA's acceptance of the self-evaluation report or agency certification of its completion. Candidate Status continues until the agency meets the required level of compliance, has been audited by a visiting committee composed of ACA auditors, and has been awarded or denied a three-year certification by the Board of Commissioners. Candidate Status lasts up to twelve months. The agency requests a standards compliance audit when the facility administrator believes the agency or facility has met or exceeded the compliance levels required for certification (100 percent mandatory, 90 percent nonmandatory).

Standards Compliance Audit

The agency's request for an audit is made six to eight weeks before the desired audit dates. The purpose of the audit is to have the visiting committee measure the agency's operation against the standards based on the documentation provided by the agency. A visiting committee completes the audit and prepares a visiting committee report for submission to the Commission. ACA designates a visiting committee chair to organize and supervise the committee's activities.

Prior to arrival at the audit site, each member of the visiting committee reviews the agency's descriptive narrative and any additional information that ACA may have provided, including pending litigation and court orders submitted by the agency and any inmate correspondence. The visiting committee chair makes audit assignments to each auditor. For example, one auditor may audit the administrative, fiscal, and personnel standards/expected practices, while another audits standards/expected practices for physical plant, sanitation, and security. Upon arrival, the visiting committee meets with the administrator, certification manager, and other appropriate staff to discuss the scope of the audit and the schedule of activities. This exchange of information provides for the development of an audit schedule that ensures the least amount of disruption to routine agency operation. The exact amount of time required to complete the audit depends on agency size, number of applicable standards/expected practices, additional facilities to be audited, and accessibility and organization of documentation.

To hasten the audit, all documentation should be clearly referenced and located where the visiting committee is to work. The certification manager's responsibilities include compiling and making accessible to all visiting committee members the standards compliance documentation and release-of-information forms for personnel and offender records. Also, staff should be notified beforehand to ensure that they are available to discuss specific issues or conduct tours of the facility for the visiting committee. During the audit, the members of the visiting committee tour the facility, review documentation prepared for each standard/expected practice, and interview staff and offenders to make compliance decisions.

The visiting committee reports its findings on the same standards-compliance checklist used by the agency in preparing its self-evaluation report. All members of the visiting committee review all mandatory standards/expected practices, all areas of noncompliance and nonapplicability, with decisions made collectively. (Final decisions on waivers can be approved only by the Commission at the time of the agency's certification hearing.)

Interviewing staff and offenders is an integral part of the audit. In addition to speaking with those who request an interview with the team, the members of the visiting committee select other individuals to interview and with whom to discuss issues. Interviews are voluntary and occur randomly throughout the audit, and those interviewed are ensured that their discussions are confidential. In addition to auditing standards/expected practices documentation, auditors will evaluate the quality of life or conditions of confinement. An acceptable quality of life is necessary for an agency to be eligible for certification. Factors that the visiting committee consider include: the adequacy and quality of programs, activities, and services available to offenders and their involvement; occurrences of disturbances, serious incidents, assaults, or violence, including their frequency and methods of dealing with them to ensure the safety of staff and offenders or juveniles; and overall physical conditions, including conditions of confinement, program space, and institutional maintenance related to sanitation, health, and safety.

At the conclusion of the audit, the visiting committee again meets with the administrator, the certification manager, and any others selected by the administrator to discuss the results of the audit. During this exit interview, the visiting committee reports the compliance tally and all findings of noncompliance and nonapplicability, as well as preliminary decisions on waivers, stating the reasons for each decision. The chair of the visiting committee then prepares and submits a copy of the visiting committee report to ACA staff within ten days of the completion of the audit. ACA staff review the report for completeness, enter the data, and within fifteen days of the audit's completion, it is submitted to the agency administrator and other members of the visiting committee for concurrence. Upon receipt of the visiting committee report, the agency has seven days to submit its written response to the report to ACA staff and all members of the visiting committee.

The Certification Hearing

The Commission on Accreditation for Corrections is responsible for rendering certification decisions and is divided into certification panels authorized to render such decisions. Panels meet separately, or with a full board meeting, and are composed of three to five commissioners. The agency is invited to have representation at the certification hearing. Unless circumstances dictate otherwise, a member of the visiting committee is not present; however, an ACA staff member does participate.

At the certification hearing, the agency representative provides information about the agency, speaks in support of its appeal and/or waiver requests, and addresses concerns the panel may have with regards to the certification application. After completing its review, the certification panel votes to award or deny certification or continue the agency in Candidate or Correspondent Status or place the agency on probation. When an agency receives a three-year certification award, a certificate with the effective date of the award is presented to the agency representative.

The Board of Commissioners may stipulate additional requirements for certification if, in its opinion, conditions exist in the facility or program that adversely affect the life, health, or safety of the staff or offenders. These requests are specific regarding activities required and timeliness for their completion. The panel advises the agency representative of all changes at the time the certification decision is made. ACA and the Commission may deny certification for insufficient standards/expected practices compliance, inadequate plans of action, or failure to meet other requirements as determined by the Commission, including, but not limited to, the conditions of confinement in a given facility. In not awarding certification, the Commission may extend an agency in Candidate Status for a specific period of time and for identified deficiencies, if in its judgment the agency is actively pursuing compliance. Those agencies denied certification, but not extended in Candidate Status, may reapply for certification after 180 days. The agency receives written notification of all decisions relative to its certification following the certification hearing.

Certified Status

During the three-year certification period, ACA requires that certified agencies submit annual statements confirming continued standards/expected practices compliance at levels necessary for certification.

The report should include the agency's progress on completing plans of action and other significant events that may affect the certification award. In addition, ACA may require accredited agencies to submit written responses to public criticism, notoriety, or patterns of complaints about agency activity that suggest a failure to maintain standards/expected practices compliance. The Association, at its own expense and with advance notice, may conduct on-site monitoring visits to verify continued standards/expected practices compliance or conditions of confinement.

Reconsideration Process

The goal of ACA's certification process is to ensure the equity, fairness, and reliability of its decisions, particularly those that constitute either denial or revocation of Certified Status. Therefore, an agency may request reconsideration of any denial or revocation of certification. However, the reasonableness of ACA's standards, criteria, and/or procedures for certification may not serve as the basis for reconsideration. A reconsideration request is based on the grounds that the adverse decision is (1) arbitrary, erratic, or otherwise in substantial disregard of the criteria and/or procedures for certification as stated by ACA, (2) based on incorrect facts or an incorrect interpretation of facts, or (3) unsupported substantial evidence. The agency submits a written request for reconsideration to ACA staff within thirty days of the adverse decision stating the basis for the request. The Commission's Executive Committee reviews the request and decides whether there is sufficient evidence to warrant a reconsideration hearing before the Board of Commissioners. The agency is notified in writing of the Executive Committee's decision.

Revocation of Certification

A certified agency that does not maintain the required levels of compliance throughout the three-year certification period, including continuous compliance with all mandatory standards/expected practices, may have its certification award revoked. The agency is notified of its deficiencies and given a specified amount of time to correct them. If the deficiencies continue, the Board of Commissioners may place the agency on Probationary Status for an additional stated period of time and require documentation of compliance. Should the agency fail to correct the deficiencies, the Board of Commissioners may revoke the agency's certification and request that the certification certificate be returned to ACA. A certified agency that has had its certification revoked for reasons of noncompliance also may use the reconsideration process.

Recertification

To ensure continuous Certified Status, certified agencies should apply for recertification approximately twelve months before the expiration of their current certification award. For detailed information on recertification, consult your ACA staff representative.

The preceding information is provided as an overview of the certification process. Additional information on specific procedures and elements of the process is available from ACA's Standards and Accreditation Department.

COMMISSION ON ACCREDITATION FOR CORRECTIONS

Executive Committee

Lannette C. Linthicum, M.D., Texas, Chair
Marge Webster, New Hampshire, Vice Chair
Kevin B. Myers, Tennessee
Denise M. Robinson, Ohio
Justin W. Jones, Oklahoma

Commissioners

Elizabeth Anderson, Washington
Lynn S. Branham, Missouri
Ronald Budzinski, Illinois
Edwin G. Buss, Indiana
Patrick J. Curran, III, Tennessee
J. David Donahue, Kentucky
Scott Haas, Kentucky
Pamela Hearn, Louisiana
Janice Hill, Florida
Robert Kennedy, New York
Al Lamberti, Florida
Cynthia Mausser, Ohio
Albert R. Murray, Georgia
Madeline K. Northrup, Ohio
Michael D. Pinson, Virginia
Marilyn Rogan, Nevada
Brad Slater, Utah
Thomas J. Stickrath, Ohio
William Thompson, Texas
Joe R. Williams, New Mexico

AMERICAN CORRECTIONAL ASSOCIATION 2008-2010

Officers

Harold W. Clarke, Massachusetts, President
Patricia L. Caruso, Michigan, Vice President
Daron Hall, Tennessee, President-Elect
Christopher Epps, Mississippi, Treasurer
Gary Maynard, Maryland, Immediate Past President
Mark H. Saunders, Maryland, Board of Governors Representative
Ana T. Aguirre, Texas, Board of Governors Representative
James A. Gondles, Jr., CAE, Executive Director

Board of Governors

Ekpe D. Ekpe, New York
Joyce Fogg, Virginia
David A. Gaspar, Arizona
Jeanna Gomez, Texas
Robert L. Guy, North Carolina
Gail M. Heller, Ohio
Lawrence E. Hicks, Oklahoma
Artis R. Hobbs, Arkansas
Mary V. Leftridge Byrd, Washington, DC
George Little, Tennessee
Mary L. Livers, Louisiana
Walter A. McFarlane, Virginia
David M. Parrish, Florida
Kathy Pittman, Mississippi
Robert Rosenbloom, Georgia
Mark H. Saunders, Maryland
Shannon D. Teague, Ohio
David L. Thomas, M.D., Florida

Standards Committee

Harley Lappin, Washington, DC, Chair
Lannette Linthicum, M.D., CCHP-A, Texas, Vice Chair
Kathleen Bachmeier, North Dakota
Jeffrey A. Beard, Pennsylvania
Ronald Budzinski, Illinois
Daniel Craig, Iowa
Brian Fischer, New York
Steve Gibson, Montana
Stanley Glanz, Oklahoma
David Haasenritter, Virginia
Justin Jones, Oklahoma
James LeBlanc, Louisiana
Mary Livers, Louisiana
Denise Robinson, Ohio
Marilyn Rogan, Nevada
Paula Smith, North Carolina
William Thompson, Texas
Marge Webster, New Hampshire

Executive Office

James A. Gondles, Jr., CAE, Executive Director
Jeffrey A. Washington, Deputy Executive Director
Jennifer Bechtel, Director, Administration and Grants
India Vargas, Senior Administrative Assistant

Standards and Accreditation Staff

Jeffrey Washington, Acting Director
Pam Eckler, Accreditation Specialist
Terri Jackson, Accreditation Specialist
Christina Randolph, Office Manager
Irawaty Bakker, Administrative Assistant
Nadine Lee, Administrative Assistant
Terry Carter, Administrative Assistant

Members of the Commission on Accreditation for Corrections 1974-2010

A

Ackermann, John (NY) 1976-1977

Anderson, Elizabeth (DC) 2002-2004, 2008-2010

B

Black, James (CO) 1986-1988*

Blake, Gary (MD) 1979-1984

Bogard, David A. (NY) 2000-2004

Borjeson, Terry (CT) 1999-2000

Boswell, Anita (AL) 2002-2004

Braithwaite, John (Canada) 1980-1986

Branham, Lynn S. (IL) 1990-1998, 2000-2002, 2008-2010

Breaux, Donald J. (LA) 1990-1996

Brown, Mel (TX) 2000-2004

Brutsche, Robert L. (VA) 1986-1998

Budzinksi, Ron (IL) 2006-2010

Buss, Edwin G. (IN) 2008-2012

C

Campbell, Donal (TN) 1999-2000

Caruso, Patricia (MI) 2003-2004

Casselbury, Parkes (FL) 2002-2004

Catley, Dan (VA) 2000-2004

Charters, Paul (FL) 1979-1984

Chin, Arleen (NH) 2000-2002

Clarke, Harold (NE) 2000-2004

Clute, Penelope D. (NY) 1984-1990

Coate, Alfred B. (MT) 1975-1980

Cocoros, John (TX) 1988-1994

Coleman, Raymond J. (WA) 1984-1990

Corsentino, Dan L. (CO) 1996-1998

Crawford, Jacqueline (AZ) 1986-1992, 2002-2004

Crosby, James V. (FL) 2001-2005

Cunningham, Su (TX) 1992-1998

Curran, Patrick J., III (TN) 2008-2012

Cushwa, Patricia (MD) 2002-2004

D

David, Monica (FL) 2004-2008

Dennehy, Kathleen M. (MA) 2004-2006

DePrato, Debra, M.D., (LA) 2004-2008

Dietz, Christopher D. (NJ) 1980-1986

Dooley, Barbara (TN) 2000-2004

Donahue, J. David (KY) 2008-2010

Dunbar, Walter (NY) 1974-1975

Dunning, James (VA) 1990-1996

Dupree, James (AL) 1996-2002

E

Elias, Al (NJ) 1979-1980

Elrod, Richard J. (IL) 1984-1986

Enomoto, J. J. (CA) 1980-1986

Epps, Christopher (MS) 2004-2008

Evans, David C. (CA) 1988-1990

F

Fant, Fred D. (NJ) 1974-1978

Farkas, Gerald M. (PA) 1974-1978

Fitzgibbons, Mark (SC) 1996-2004

Frawley, Michael H. (MO) 1996-2002

Fryer, Gordon L. (IL) 1974-1978

G

Garvey, Robert (MA) 2000-2004

George, B. James, Jr. (NY) 1979-1984

Ghee, Margarette (OH) 1996-2004

Gladstone, William E. (FL) 1981-1986

Goodrich, Edna L. (WA) 1978-1982

Goord, Glenn (NY) 2002-2006

Green, Leslie R. (MN) 1979-1984

H

Haas, Scott (KY) 2008-2012

Hamden, Michael (NC) 1999-2004

Hamilton, William (OH) 2000-2004

Hammergren, Donald R. (MN) 1975-1979

Hattaway, George (TN) 1995-1996

Hays, Bonnie L. (OR) 1987-1992

Heard, John (TX) 1974-1978

Hearn, Pamela (LA) 2006-2010

Hegmann, M.D., Michael (LA) 1999-2000

Heyne, Robert P. (IN) 1974-1977

Hill, Janice (FL) 2006-2010

Hill-Christian, Sheila (VA) 1996-2004

Hofacre, Robert (OH) 2000-2004

Holcomb, Beth (VA) 2002-2006

Hopkins, Wayne (DC) 1974-1977

Huggins, M. Wayne (VA) 1983-1988*

I

Irving, James R. (IL) 1981-1986

J

Jackson, Ron (TX) 1990-1996

Jackson, Ronald W. (GA) 1992-1998

Jefferson, Ralph A. (WI) 1978-1983

Johnson, Perry M. (MI) 1986-1992

Jones, Justin W. (OK) 2008-2010

Jordan, James M. (IL) 1984-1996

K

Kehoe, Charles J. (VA) 1983-1988

Kennedy, Robert (NY) 2006-2010

Keohane, Patrick (MO) 1999-2000

Kinker, Jeannette (NM) 2000-2002, 2004-2008